Women Who Win

By Mary C. Crowley

Think Mink!
Women Who Win

WOMEN WHO WIN

MARY C. CROWLEY

Fleming H. Revell
A Division of Baker Book House
Grand Rapids, Michigan 49516

Unless otherwise identified, all Scripture quotations are from The Living Bible, Copyright © 1971 by Tyndale House Publishers, Wheaton, Illinois 60187.
Scripture quotations identified KJV are from the King James Version of the Bible.

The poem "The Challenge" by Dr. Heartsill Wilson is used by permission of the author.
"The Source of Power in Our Lives" by S. M. Lockridge is used by permission of the author.

Library of Congress Cataloging in Publication Data

Crowley, Mary C
   Women who win.

   1. Success. 2. Women executives—United States.
3. Women—Religious lives. I. Title.
HF5386.C897   658.4'0092'2   79-11390
ISBN 0-8007-0993-4

Twenty-sixth printing, March 1993

Printed in the United States of America

Contents

Preface

WORDS . . . WORDS . . . WORDS

All around us—there are *words* being beamed at the American woman.

Words from magazines—
Words from books—
Words from television—
Words from seminars for women—

all urging women to find their identity—learn to be aggressive—learn to be assertive—all perhaps well meaning but confusing. Instead of helping women to find identity, all the words have persistently challenged everything *female* and have contributed to a severe identity crisis among American women.

It has been my experience in working with thousands of women over the past thirty years that women have begun to question *who they are—what is their real role?* And they ask themselves, "Is there a Creator God? What did *He* intend for me to be?"

I believe we all need a word from God.

May these words of wisdom from God supply part of the answer.

MARY C. CROWLEY

1

A Mountaintop Experience

In everything you do, put God first, and he will direct you and crown your efforts with success.

Proverbs 3:6

The telephone was ringing. I had already finished studying awhile in Proverbs and praying for each one of the twenty-five beautiful women who waited in the lower level of our mountain lodge. Thank goodness, I had prayed also for *myself*. There are never enough hours in the day when I go to our mountain lodge in Colorado for a retreat with our company's new managers.

It has been our practice for eight years to bring our new managers to the place which was built for this purpose. We share, learn, eat, shop, play, laugh, and pray together. Part of our study is about how we women can become competent leaders in our business, more effective managers in our homes, and more fulfilled individuals in the total role of today's woman.

In pursuing these aspirations, we go to the greatest Source of all for our teaching. We have not found a better source book than the one Pat Boone calls the "manufacturer's handbook"—God's own Book, the Holy Bible.

For our Bible study we use Proverbs in learning how to become wise and effective leaders. We have classes on the techniques and skills of leadership, incorporating the wisdom of Proverbs into our lesson material.

I've found that God can accomplish more in my life if I give Him a portion of my time to start the day. It looked as though He would have to work overtime on this November morning. The sun had barely chased away the shadows from the side of Mount Princeton and already the telephone was ringing.

I picked up the receiver to hear Peaches Mathews, my faithful assistant at our Dallas headquarters. Peaches's words were full of awe. "Mrs. *C,* the Office of the President of the United States just called. You have been asked to go to the White House on Thursday for a conference with him and the Chiefs of Staff."

The President . . . ? Thursday . . . ?

I struggled to get my schedule in focus. Thursday was two days away. It was the day I was scheduled to speak to the Christian Women's Club of Buena Vista at a luncheon meeting. There was much excitement over the special occasion and already over 280 women were planning to come.

I, too, was excited. I realized that there were many women in the valley who needed a wonderful, exciting, positive Christian message—needed to be made to feel like a "somebody." I had really looked forward to being with them. In addition, the twenty-five new managers in our company were to be my guests all week, Thursday included.

Now what was all this talk about the White House?

"Peaches," I said slowly, "would you just run that by again?"

"It's the Executive Office," Peaches said. "President Carter has invited twenty-five heads of businesses from across the nation to meet with him and his Chiefs of Staff to discuss current business trends and leadership input. You are one of the leaders he has invited."

So it *was* the President! Well, that was wonderful, of course. But surely he didn't think I could just drop everything and run to Washington!

"You'll have to tell them I am too busy right now," I said hesitantly. "See if Don or Barbara might represent us." (Don Carter is our executive vice-president and my wonderful son. Barbara Hammond is the assistant sales manager and company vice-president.)

Still in a whirl, I hurried downstairs to where my managers were waiting with their Bibles, tablets, and tape recorders. We'd spent yesterday morning learning how the wisdom of Proverbs could enable us to become effective leaders. Today, and every other morning during the week, we would continue. In the past, hundreds of other women had come to the mountain to study ways of becoming more effective leaders and career women as well as better homemakers and mothers. They'd gone back to their homes all over America, fired with the spiritual energy that is needed to meet the demands of home, husband, and career.

I wanted these women, also, to become winners. Not even a call from the President of the United States could stand in the way.

I looked around the room. There were the young women, still in their twenties, with preschoolers to care for and husbands struggling to advance in their careers. There were mothers in the thirties and forties with teenagers to motivate in a topsy-turvy world, while they themselves sought greater fulfillment. And there were grandmothers filling their empty nests with the excitement of a new career.

This morning we were going to talk about putting God first. But first I wanted to tell them about the phone call.

"An interesting thing just happened," I said. "The Office of the President of the United States just called, inviting me to come to Washington on Thursday. I had to tell them to say I was just too busy to come."

Mouths dropped open. Eyes grew large. Everyone began talking at once. "You can't do that," they all seemed to be saying. "You must go. We'll manage. We want you to go and represent us to the President."

"But how about the study in Proverbs and the speech at the Christian Women's Luncheon? I can't just pick up and leave!" I protested.

"Of course you can," they all chimed at once. "We'll do the program for the luncheon."

"I really think we need God's guidance on this," I said. "I want to be where *He* wants me. Let's pray about it." As is our custom, we joined hands and formed a friendship prayer circle in front of the crackling fireplace. As we asked for God's guidance, I felt His wonderful peace clearing away the confusion in my mind. Calmed down a bit, we all sat down and opened our Bibles and had a rewarding study time.

We study Proverbs because it is part of the wisdom literature. The Proverbs consist of insights and admonitions that enable us to better serve God in daily living. It is a book written by King Solomon to his sons to teach them how to be leaders. It teaches people how to live responsibly and to act wisely in all circumstances, for Solomon wanted his sons to be *understanding, just,* and *fair* in everything they did. King Solomon writes that he wanted those already wise to become even wiser and to become leaders through exploring the depths of meaning in these bits of wisdom and truth.

Each new manager is given a leather-bound Living Bible with her

name on it. The Living Bible is a paraphrase of the King James transla-
tion and, being written in today's language, is a good way to begin in
studying God's Word.

As we were finishing our Bible study, the phone rang again. It was
Peaches. "Mrs. *C,* the President doesn't want anyone else from Home
Interiors and Gifts. He wants you," she insisted.

Then Don was on the phone. He was brief, businesslike, and to the
point. "I have arranged for the company plane to pick you up tomorrow afternoon at five. You'll be in Washington tomorrow night and all
day Thursday, and back Thursday evening. You will be here for Fri-
day."

It was settled. And the peace that I felt about it made me realize that
it was God's direction in answer to our prayer.

On Wednesday we crammed two days' study into one, planned the
program for Thursday, and got me ready for a trip to visit the President. By 5 P.M. I was in Salida, Colorado where the Home Interiors' jet
waited to fly me to the nation's Capital. As I watched the snowcapped
Colorado mountains fade into the sunset, it seemed unreal that I was
going to Washington, D.C., as a guest of the President of the United
States!

Years ago, when I had struggled alone to support my two preschoolers, such a thing would have seemed preposterous! In those days of
kids, meals, laundry, and bills, I would never have dreamed that my
opinion could ever count for very much *anywhere.* And this trip would
have been beyond my wildest imagination.

But our lives are often like that as women. We run in circles. There
are children, husbands, homes. There is community, church, Little
League. There are sports events, taxi service, music. So many demands. . . . If we do not have a good, solid anchor we will be pulled
apart and our emotions will end up ragged, our dispositions frazzled.

But when God is our anchor, somehow that circle becomes a spiral,
ever broadening and taking in more people and more opportunities,
making more room for joy and fulfillment.

In Ecclesiastes we are told that there is a time to be born and a time
to die; a time to plant and a time to harvest; a time to kill and a time to
heal. And for a woman, the right timing is essential. There is a time to
nurture children and a time to let them go; a time to stay home and a
time to seek a career; a time to devote herself to others and a time to
think of herself.

God's wisdom teaches us to observe priorities and to do things in the right timing is essential. There is a time to nurture children and a time to let them go; a time to stay home and a time to seek a career; a time to devote herself to others and a time to think of herself.

God's wisdom teaches us to observe priorities and to do things in the right timing. His Word tells us that if we trust Him and lean not on our own understanding—if we put Him first in our lives—with His help and guidance there is no limit to what we can do.

Recently at the convention of the Direct Sales Association some of the presidents of other companies had asked how we managed to attract such enlightened, attractive, feminine leaders for Home Interiors and Gifts.

"We grow them," I answered proudly. And it was true. More than one shy, insecure woman had come into our organization, hoping to make some extra money. She had found that and more. She had found confidence, a new way of life, and a trust in the Lord that brought her the immeasurable riches of self-fulfillment. She had become an inspiration to her family and a model for others.

How unfortunate that every woman in America does not have the same opportunity to learn to be a fulfilled woman and a leader in her community. It would be so wonderful if every woman could have the same opportunities that we are able to make possible for so many. If women only knew how much they matter to God, they would not find it necessary to go out into the world and assert themselves in a negative and unattractive way. If they could know of God's plan for their lives, so many of their problems would be solved!

Surely every woman can benefit from a study of Proverbs. Throughout this book, we will be sharing with you, women who have benefited from the study and practice of Proverbs: *Women Who Win*. Here is one who writes with authority and experience. She is vice-president of sales management with twenty-five thousand saleswomen and sometimes more. Barbara Hammond has been with Home Interiors several years and is now in the highest position of vice-president and assistant sales manager with the supervision, training, and management of over twenty-five thousand independent saleswomen—a *real* winner in every sense.

What a source of revelation and deep strength it was for me the day I came to know—really know—that in addition to being a wife and mother of two beautiful children, God's plan for my life included a leadership role in our beloved Home Interiors and Gifts.

How grateful I am that, along with my rather shy, quiet personality, God also instilled in me the ability to have faith and trust and to be led by my leaders. . . . I have learned to submit to authority without surrendering my own identity . . . and as Mary C trained me through the years to grow into what I am becoming today . . . constantly I could bolster my personal sense of worth through the teaching of Proverbs.

Proverbs 10:13 says, in part, "Men with common sense are admired as counselors. . . ." Proverbs 16:21: "The wise man is known by his common sense, and a pleasant teacher is the best."

I realized no amount of book learning or higher education (of which I have little) could replace the D.C.S. Degree–Degree of Common Sense–and how I pray for this daily as I work with our people.

Hatred stirs old quarrels, but **love** *overlooks insults.*
                              Proverbs 10:12 (italics mine)

How this verse has lifted me, for I know love given to our family, friends, and business associates strengthens them and builds confidence . . . . In return, love comes back 100 fold.

And at times, when I think I am too quiet in certain situations . . . I remember Proverbs 10:14:

A wise man holds his tongue. Only a fool blurts out everything he knows; that only leads to sorrow and trouble.

I then know that in business situations to speak only when I have something worthwhile to say.

These are but four of the verses in Proverbs that have sustained me and given me wisdom to grow.

How precious and meaningful it is, as I have now grown to an executive position in our company that it is—in a sense—a fulfillment of what we read in Proverbs 31 where we, as working women, are given God's badge of approval.

My everlasting goal would be to develop into God's ideal woman described in this Proverb.

Her children stand and bless her . . . .

2

Wisdom and Common Sense

Have two goals: wisdom—that is, knowing and doing right— and common sense. . . .

Proverbs 3:21

Without wise leadership, a nation is in trouble; but with good counselors there is safety.

Proverbs 11:14

For the reverence and fear of God are basic to all wisdom. Knowing God results in every other kind of understanding.

Proverbs 9:10

Had I been here before? Fascinated, I stared at the huge oval table ringed by chairs, which bore the names of the cabinet members on the backs. How many times had I watched on television as the President of the United States signed a bill or received a prime minister in this very room! And now I was not seeing the Oval Office on television—I was there! I could actually smell the polish on the dark wood paneling. Thinking of all the important matters that had been resolved in this very room, I felt very much a part of history. Glancing around at the twenty-one men and the three other women who also were guests of the President—all of them heads of large American companies—I could not help but wonder if they, too, shared my excitement.

We waited expectantly, having been put at ease by our President's

17

kind assistant. Then, suddenly, the door opened. And as we all rose to our feet President Carter strode into the room, wearing his famous smile. He gave each of us a warm handshake, calling us by name, before taking his place at the large oval table.

Before there was really any time for conversation or getting acquainted, an army of reporters and television cameramen burst into the room and began thrusting microphones at the President and hurling questions at him. I felt compassion for him. It seemed that he really could not make any wise answers amid all the confusion and the lights and noise—there was not time to really study the questions. I realized some of the difficulties that public figures surely must have, being so abruptly thrust, without preamble, into every home in the nation by way of television. They, after all, are human, too.

Once the press had left we all got down to business. We met the different cabinet heads and heard a short talk by each one. Then the President spoke. He told us that the nation had three major problems: unemployment, the national debt, and the energy crisis. He wanted to know how we felt our companies could help.

We, in turn, had a chance to discuss some of our problems with him. There was no way, we told him, that American businesses could save energy and, at the same time, enlarge businesses in order to hire more workers, to provide more jobs.

We asked questions that did not seem to have answers. The cabinet members did not seem to have the answers either. Each one seemed not to know what was going on outside his own department. I was again reminded of the many problems in our nation that stem from this bureaucracy, this tremendous lack of coordination.

I had to remind myself that Paul said in the thirteenth chapter of Romans that God gave us the law and that the administration of the law is according to His plan; that all authority is from God. Yet I did not agree with everything the President had to say. He was doing his very best. But the problems were serious, and our government hopelessly complicated. Certainly our President needed wisdom far beyond his years or his experience.

These were the thoughts that churned in my mind as the Home Interiors' plane whisked me back across our vast nation that evening. What could *I* do, I wondered.

And suddenly I knew. I could pray. Pray for the President to surround himself with good counselors. Pray that he would receive wisdom from above. I could pray for the President and I could enlist others to do likewise. If all of the millions of dedicated Christians in the United States would pray that our leaders would seek God's wisdom, what wonderful changes could come about in America!

I remembered that the course of a nation's history had once been changed when one woman had prayed, and had then acted on God's answer. I thought of my Old Testament model and friend, that woman who was a judge, Deborah, whom God told us about in the Book of Judges. I remembered how her story ends with the promise of national rest and peace for forty years.

Yes, prayers had changed the course of history. And they still could! Right away I resolved to enlist our Home Interiors' people to pray regularly for the President and for his administration.

Outside the darkened window the lights of one small town after another appeared on the horizon, twinkling like diamonds, then faded into the blackness of the night. Down there were millions of Americans who had to live by the decisions made by our government. They faced inflation, possible unemployment, energy shortage. And in addition, they were confronted with the difficult decisions necessitated by the demands of daily living. Most were struggling to support families. Many were trying just to get along. Lots were lonely, weary. Thousands were the victims of disease or drugs or alcohol.

Along with all our wonderful opportunities as a nation, we had many problems. Crime, pornography, child abuse, inflation . . . the list was endless, even in this great land and under the greatest system of government in the world.

How much tragedy could be avoided if only each of us really knew that our Heavenly Father cares for us, wants to lead and guide us, longs for fellowship with us! But even God cannot give us more than we are mentally, spiritually, and emotionally prepared to receive.

For the reverence and fear of God are basic to all wisdom, King Solomon had said. *Knowing God results in every other kind of understanding.*

Reverence. How we all need that kind of worshipful submission to God that opens the way for miracles in our lives. *The fear of God.* Not a skulking terror, but a glorious respect and awe that we experience in the presence of the Almighty God who created the universe, who flung the stars into space—and yet who loves each of us and desires fellowship with us.

I often remember the words of my friend Dr. Clyde Narramore, well-known Christian psychologist, who says, "Every person is worth understanding." But in order to understand others we must first understand ourselves with God-given wisdom and insight. The only way we can ever really love and understand one another and build relationships that last—the only way we can truly understand ourselves and our real potential is to first know and love and revere God.

And all women everywhere have a need for understanding, for guidance, for wisdom. All women, no matter how lowly or how exalted their state in life, have a need for a relationship with a God who understands woman, because He created woman and made her to be the special creature that she is.

Several years ago I took a poll of the thousands of women who were attending Home Interiors' Rallies all across America. I asked each woman to list the one characteristic which she wanted more of in the three key areas of her life: home and family, business and career, and community and social life. Interestingly, the one trait these women most needed and desired was a *better self-image* and a greater feeling of self-confidence. Even in this enlightened and prosperous land of ours, many women just do not feel confident and capable. They do not "feel like somebody."

It was at that point that I began to try to teach women to become "somebodies," telling them that "God doesn't take the time to make a nobody." I was determined to help each woman with whom I came in contact to learn to think like a winner, to feel like a winner, to "be a somebody."

And now we have over twenty-five thousand marvelous "somebodies" in this company—women who have learned through our teaching to put their priorities in order; who have learned that their self-worth is related to the character of the God who designed and created them—women who have learned to know and love and trust their Heavenly Father.

Many are still learning. We try to develop an atmosphere of love that will provide for individual growth and our Heavenly Father—amazingly—does the rest.

I feel such a compassion for the many women who are devoted to the Women's Liberation movement. They are trying to win, but in the wrong way. And yet I can understand much of their motivation. I recall the university program in which I was a member of a panel discussing the future of women. One of the other panel members, an aggressive career woman, demanded to know why I was not working actively in the movement, since I was obviously convinced that women could and should be leaders.

"I believe in helping women to find dignity and status through their own success, rather than demanding that it be given to them by legislation," I told her.

"You are just ignorant!" she shouted, pointing an accusing finger at me.

"We are all ignorant," I replied quietly. "Only about different things." Angrily, she picked up her chair and moved it as far away from me as possible. My heart really ached for her. She had a worthy cause but her methods were self-defeating.

I believe women are special, that God created us to be special. Our Code of Ethics at Home Interiors and Gifts says it best: *We believe in the dignity and the importance of women. We believe that everything a woman touches should be ennobled by that touch.*

I don't think we women need to be more aggressive. And I certainly do not believe in being a doormat. I want every woman to have an abundance of self-confidence—to feel like somebody. I want women to *like* themselves and to have self-confidence.

But I also want women to be beautiful, feminine, charming, gracious and wise—for this is what God intended.

When King Solomon wrote the Book of Proverbs long before the birth of Jesus Christ, he had the same dream for his people. He wanted to make the "simpleminded" unlearned wise. He wanted those already wise to become even wiser, to become leaders by exploring the depths of eternal truth.

Exploring truth takes commitment and discipline. Like precious stones, these treasures are not just sprinkled around everywhere. One must dig and search, read and study. And one must pray. God's Word, the Bible, is the source of all wisdom and truth, but to the locked heart it is a locked Book. Yet, for the sincere and diligent there are treasures of wisdom to be found. And in the Book of Proverbs in particular there are many excellent guidelines for developing real leadership qualities.

Do you crave greater fulfillment in your home, in your career, in your community life? Do you want to know yourself better and like yourself more? Do you desire to understand God's plan for your life? Then study Proverbs. Set aside some time each day to read and study what God has to say to people who want to learn. Pray that God will grant you His wisdom.

Remember, you can be a *somebody*. You can be a leader. You can be the person that God wants you to be!

Here is a gracious successful woman who shares with you what God has done in her life. Pearl Burns is Area Manager and leader of nearly five thousand women in sales and management, effective citizen in her community, involved in civic and church affairs and yet, having her priorities in order. Pearl's early life was turned toward spiritual things by a precious godly grandmother, but it was in January of 1970 (after being in Home Interiors for eleven years) that Pearl made a total commitment of her life, home, career, and material success to the Lord.

Pearl Burns says it this way:

Our Lord Jesus Has a Great Plan for My Life. If I am going to successfully lead, I must be willing to be led. What a great way to learn from God Himself, as I study the Book of Proverbs.

I have been made aware of the importance that our Lord Jesus wants to teach, show, instruct, and discipline me. If God is to use my life, I must be obedient to what Jesus tells me.

The confidence that I have gained in leading others has come as a result of my believing in Him and trying my best to follow His advice. As long as I listen to what God says, I am on safe ground. Before our Lord can use me effectively, I must ask Him for cleansing; then He can show me and use me as a witness to share the Good News.

The Book of Proverbs is a confirmation to me that I must keep my eyes on the Christ of the Cross where Jesus fulfilled the Scriptures— and in His Word which gives me the practical plan for daily living. Our studies in Proverbs keep me reminded of the How to live effectively and positively in a negative world.

Mary Crowley has been a perfect example of Christian leadership that every person would want to follow. Once in your lifetime, you have the opportunity to meet a leader like Mary, who exemplifies the love of our Lord Jesus, a leader who walks the walk. What a joy to share this tremendous way of life with others! To God be the Glory!

3

God's Four Rs of Learning

Reverence for God adds hours to each day. . . .
Proverbs 10:27

While growing up we sometimes heard of the three *R*s of learning: *readin'*, *'ritin'* and *'rithmetic*. In Proverbs, however, we have the Bible's four *R*s of learning: *reverence, respect, responsibility* and *reward*.

I know many people who reverence the Lord in a distant and remote way but who have not yet learned to trust Him in a personal relationship. Indeed, many do not realize that it is possible to know God personally. How I want each of them to know the joy and excitement of trusting Him completely.

Sometimes we forget the opportunities that are ours to learn and grow. When I first met Nancy Good, she was shy, scared, and insecure—she was a new mother and unsure of her ability in some areas of life. She is now a confident Area Manager, mother and wife—says, *Let's just Praise the Lord!*

Praise Be to God for the opportunity to learn, think and love.

In the studying of Proverbs, we find common sense mentioned as important for all of us. The Lord has been so helpful to me in the area of common sense. Many, many times He has said, "Nancy, use what I have given you" when a situation needs attention. God says to make decisions prayerfully–oh, the lessons He teaches if we open our minds to learn!

"The Lord demands fairness in every business deal. He estab-lished this principle" (Proverbs 16:11). Amazing that the Lord knew years ago that business people needed that bit of wisdom. We in

*business must use God's wisdom, trust in Him, and try to be the leader He expects us to be. I do not know **how** without His daily guidance! The study of Proverbs brings to all of us a pattern of daily living. What a challenge and what a glorious reminder the cross is—that He died so we can all be saved—even if we err throughout our lives. Just ask with a meaningful heart and He answers.*

God tells us that we can know Him only through His Son, Jesus. He says that when we confess our sins and ask Him to forgive us and cleanse us from all our guilt, He will do just that. He will save us from sin and death and give us a brand-new nature, and He will write our names down in the Lamb's Book of Life. He tells us that, even though many people think that we are all children of God, we are not *His* children, until we have come to Him through faith in Jesus, His Son. Because of our sin nature, we are children of this world and of the devil, until we repent and are born again into God's kingdom.

How can we be sure that we have done this successfully? Jesus tells us that when we have called on Him, He will accept us. He will come to us and make His abode with us (live in us) and manifest Himself to us. That means that we will know by our own experience that He lives with us and in us and, as we continue to walk in faith and obedience, we will feel His presence all the time. The Bible says that God gives us the Holy Spirit to indwell us as the earnest (or guarantee) of our inheritance. The Holy Spirit guides and motivates us and gives us the desire and the strength to do that which is pleasing to our Heavenly Father.

How wonderful to be a child of God through faith in Jesus, His Son. And Jesus is the only way; there is no other. If there were any other way to come to God, then Jesus' death on the cross for the sins of mankind would have been a waste.

How grateful I am to my grandparents that they helped me from the time I was a baby to know that Jesus was my Friend. Even so, in time I had to receive Him by my own decision, as my Lord and Savior. If you are not already a child of God through faith in Jesus, God wants to adopt you as His very own! No matter who you are or where you came from or what you have done, He loves you and offers you the possibility of a new life of joy and victory, here and now!

In my previous book *Think Mink!* I told how I was sent, at the age of six and a half, from the warm Christian atmosphere of my grandparents' home to live with my father and a stepmother I didn't even know in another state far away. I was miserable and lonely. But I could always enter my own private chapel in the sweet-smelling piney woods on the slopes of the rugged mountains. There I would often cry and talk to Jesus, my Friend, and even then His love and peace would surround me and lift me up.

Trusting God does not mean that we don't ever have any problems. But God is greater than anything that can ever happen to us and He goes through it all with us. Those of us who truly know Him as Father would rather go through the worst with Him than through the best without Him.

Wisdom begins with *reverence* for God. Then, after reverence, comes *respect* for the people whom God has placed in authority over us for our guidance and protection. This includes our parents, teachers, pastors, and government officials, for the Bible tells us to remember that whenever we remove ourselves from under authority, we are removing ourselves from under the umbrella of protection—whether it be divine, civil, or domestic. God has given certain other people authority over us and He has likewise charged them with the responsibility for our protection. Authority and responsibility go hand in hand.

> Listen to your father and mother. . . .
>
> Proverbs 1:9

Next is our *responsibility* to God, once He has made Himself known to us. Our Heavenly Father never demands anything from us until He has first revealed Himself to us. Then, after we have come to know Him, He gently reminds us that, as His children, we have a responsibility to Him. And everything God tells us to do, or not to do, is designed by our Heavenly Father to ensure our peace, prosperity, safety, and tranquility, as well as long life and good health.

Let's talk about prosperity. Many people do not realize that God intends for His people to be prosperous! In fact, He even tells us how to be prosperous.

> Honor the Lord by giving him the first part of all your income, and he will fill your barns with wheat and barley and overflow your wine vats with the finest wines.
>
> Proverbs 3:9, 10

In Solomon's time, full barns and overflowing wine vats were signs of prosperity. And that is what God promises to those who will put Him first and honor Him with their firstfruits, or our tithe. If we will do this, God says in the Book of Malachi, He will open the windows of heaven for us and pour out a blessing so great, that we won't even be able to handle it! And that is quite a promise!

Tithing always reminds me of my precious grandfather. I lived with my grandparents when I was a small child. They were godly, hardworking farm people and I learned many wonderful things from them.

My grandfather did not plant or harvest or do any work at all on the Sabbath, other than that which was absolutely necessary. Of course, we had to milk the cows and care for our farm animals, but Sunday was a day of worship, fellowship, and rest. Grandfather tithed not only his income, but his time as well.

The man on the neighboring farm never darkened the door of the church. Every time we drove by his place on the way to worship, he would be plowing or planting or harvesting, just the same as any other day.

On our farms in northwest Arkansas we raised Concord grapes. One particular Sunday as we drove to church we saw this farmer harvesting his grape crop. The very next day a big hailstorm demolished every cluster of the purple fruit ripening on the vines of the churchgoing farmers. Our non-Christian friend had himself a big laugh and wrote a letter to the editor of our paper, gloating that he had reaped a good harvest because he had *not* gone to church, while the Christian farmers, who had been at services, lost their entire crops!

The editor published his letter, but added the following admonition: "God doesn't settle all of His accounts in the month of October." The farmer had harvested grapes, but he had not harvested the joy of living.

What things are most important to you? What do you love? On what things have you set your affections?

> Above all else, guard your affections. For they influence everything else in your life.
>
> Proverbs 4:23

Here we learn that the things which are most cherished in our lives are those which will ultimately determine our attitudes and goals, our life-styles and our behavior. How important it is, then, that we choose very carefully the things that are to be utmost in our affections, remembering that Jesus warned us that where our treasures are, our hearts would be also. When we choose to set our affections on things above, as God has commanded us, we gain an eternal security that cannot be destroyed. Then, after these priorities are resolved, the way is open to receive all the blessings that God promised to those who faithfully put Him first in their lives.

> In everything you do, put God first, and he will direct you and crown your efforts with success. Don't be conceited, sure of your own wisdom. Instead, trust and reverence the Lord, and turn your back on evil. . . .
>
> Proverbs 3:6, 7

This is the wisdom that is from above. It lies in knowing that each new day is a gift from God and an opportunity for which to thank Him. We thank Him, too, for life and breath and health, for family and loved ones. We ask for His help, His guidance, in every situation and we bring all our problems—rebellion, jealousy, fatigue, impatience—to Him. God is our Father and He expects us to call home regularly, collect and person-to-person! He is always there. And He is never too busy to hear from us.

We've talked about some of God's *R*s—reverence, respect, and responsibility. But there is another very important one: *reward*. Let's see what God promises in His holy Word, the Bible, to those who are His faithful children.

Here is a beautiful illustration of the rewards of the here and now for women who win with God. Beverly Channell is an Area Manager with Home Interiors, living in Omaha, Nebraska, and has been associated with us for fourteen years. When we first met Beverly she was a student in El Paso; then, briefly, was a frustrated school teacher in California. Beverly felt she needed a creative outlet and started in Home Interiors on a part-time basis. That would allow her still to be mother to two children and wife to Bill. Bill was transferred often and it was difficult for Beverly. She found the right "growth" atmosphere through the plan of love and program of study of management in Home Interiors and decided to leave teaching and come with us full time. Hear the words of Beverly Channell:

> *"If I had my life to live over . . . and knew what I know now . . . !"*
> *How many times have you heard that statement made?*
> *And yet, life is a preparatory growing experience. During it, God brings us–through situations, and under the influence of other*

people—to fulfillment of the potential He has created within each of us. Yes, God has a plan for each of us.

From the study of Proverbs, it has been amazing to me to realize the wealth of wisdom and many practical applications to be found for personal growth, for everyday relationships, and for business.

There are no secrets to success—but God-inspired principles of understanding people, of wisdom in judgments, of diligence in service, and of following instructions.

Trust in the Lord with all thine heart; and lean not unto thine own understanding. In all thy ways acknowledge him, and he shall direct thy paths.

Proverbs 3:5, 6 KJV

In retrospect, it is easy for me to see how God has kept His hand over me and has blessed me with a loving family, and has further cultivated me for a role of leadership in our company, Home Interiors. I have realized a growing insight, responsibility, and influence in my life far beyond what might have been my highest aspirations.

Here I have known a climate for growth and have had the vehicle for touching the lives of many people as mine has been touched by the living philosophy of Mary Crowley and other associates who have enriched my life.

My prayer is that my life will continue to be a blessing to others, and that I will continue to learn from the principles and promises of His Word.

Being confident of this very thing, that he which hath begun a good work in you will perform it until the day of Jesus Christ.

Philippians 1:6 KJV

4

What Will Be Our Reward?

He grants good sense to the godly . . . .

Proverbs 2:7

Wisdom gives: A long, good life, Riches, Honor, Pleasure, Peace.

Proverbs 3:16, 17

What will be our reward? God tells us in His Word that if we put Him first and seek His wisdom He will reward us with His guidance, good sense, success, a long, good life, riches, honor, pleasure, and peace. These are God's promises to us.

Can you think of anything else to ask for?

Perhaps you are thinking that you know many dedicated Christians, who do indeed reverence God, but who are nevertheless living in poverty or nearly so. Or possibly you can recall God-fearing people who have suffered terrible disease or have died young. How can Proverbs tell us to expect a long life and riches when we can see just the opposite happening to many who have put God first in their lives?

God's promises of reward are real. But it is necessary to view them from God's perspective and not from our own. For He is faithful, and will always give us the blessings He has promised, or something even better, when we honor Him and put our trust in Him. Let's look at some of these promised rewards and see how God would define them.

A good, long life. Do these words refer to the number of years you live? Do they refer to the luxury of your surroundings? God's values are eternal. His definition of a good, long life is one that is devoted to His service.

I am reminded of my son-in-law's nephew, Todd—a darling Christian boy of fifteen who loved sports and played on the school soccer team. In May of 1977, Todd and his father went scuba diving together. They had looked forward to the adventure of deep diving together and were having the time of their lives in the water, until Todd's father suddenly realized his son was missing. Along with others, he plunged again and again into the murky waters to search for Todd, with no success. When at last he was found, it was too late. The boy had drowned.

Seemingly, such a tragedy! Many people wondered that day how God could allow the death of a precious boy of fifteen, who seemed to have such promise. But the answer came in the message of Mel Carter, the assistant pastor of our church, who spoke at Todd's memorial service.

"We all think of a full life as three score and ten," he said, "and for many it is. Yet, God must look at time lives in a completely different way. According to the message of God's Word, anyone who brings others to know God and promotes a greater longing for Jesus has lived a fulfilled life."

Arriving at the graveside, we noticed a large group of teenagers from Todd's school. The scene we were soon to witness would serve to indicate that Todd had indeed brought others to Christ, even in death. In the midst of the mourners stood Todd's grandmother, her arms around two teenage girls—friends of Todd. Suddenly both girls fell to their knees among the flowers surrounding the casket, which held Todd's earthly remains, and dedicated their lives to the Lord, whom Todd had loved and served. God consoled us in a beautiful way by putting a special blessing on that time. And because of Todd's life, other young people made dedications and commitments to the Lord that day as well.

From God's viewpoint, Todd's life was full and complete although brief in time. And because Todd was a Christian his life goes on eternally!

The poet Longfellow says in *A Psalm of Life!*

> Lives of great men all remind us
> We can make our lives sublime.
> And, departing, leave behind us
> Footprints on the sands of time.

What kind of footprints am I leaving? What kind do your feet make? What kind would you like to make? God's definition of a good life—a long life—is different from ours. We measure in years; He measures in eternal values.

Riches. What kind of riches do you work for? Do you crave Cadillacs or contented children? Diamonds, or the desire and ability to serve others? God is fully capable of rewarding you with the Cadillacs *and* the diamonds, but there are greater blessings to be had—blessings which give much greater joy. And many of them are blessings that are too often taken for granted!

All truly successful people have several things in common. They have definite values, goals, and purposes; they are enthusiastic and persistent. They have put God first, and their chief aim is to render service to others. Money is only a secondary consideration.

> The Lord's blessing is our greatest wealth. All our work adds
> nothing to it!
>
> Proverbs 10:22

I once knew a very wise man who understood that lesson very well. He and his wife once listened to a very rich and successful banker speak at a convention banquet. As they applauded the speaker when he had finished, the wife gently patted her husband's hand. "That's all right, honey," she said reassuringly. "Someday we'll be every bit as rich as he is."

Her husband turned to her, smiling. "We're rich now," he said quietly. "And someday we'll have money."

Jesus reminds us that the quality of a man's life does not consist in the abundance of the things which he possesses. Scriptures remind us again and again of the folly of putting our confidence in material wealth. On the other hand, we are exhorted to lay up for ourselves treasures in heaven—treasures that cannot rot or decay or be stolen from us. God reminds us that where our treasure is, there our hearts will be. And He wants us to be sure that our hearts are in a safe place where we cannot be hurt or disappointed.

> If you work for the things you believe in
>   You are *rich,* though the way is rough—
> If you work only for money
>   You can never make quite enough.

Honor.

> Honor goes to kind and gracious women, mere money to cruel
> men.
>
> Proverbs 11:16

This Scripture does not mean that all women are kind and gracious
nor that all men are cruel. It merely stresses the fact that honor will go
to the kind and gracious—to those who earn the respect of others by
their kind and gracious behavior.

Pleasure. What *is* pleasure? Television commercials would have us
believe that pleasure comes from something you can eat or drink.
Magazine ads suggest that pleasure can be had in a particular brand of
cigarette. We are often tempted to think that pleasure is to be found in a
sweet dessert, a luxurious vacation trip, an expensive car, a more
comfortable mattress. But the best that any of these things can offer is
short-term pleasure—some even with long-term and undesirable af-
tereffects.

The old Pennsylvania Dutch saying "It pleasures me" indicates a
long-term pleasant feeling. That's the kind of joy Proverbs is talking
about: the joy that comes from a life of dedication and service. There is
much pleasure in just being with others in worship. And the greatest
joy of all is a close, personal relationship with God.

Peace. We are told in the Scriptures that the only real peace is the
peace of God, and that God's peace is beyond human understanding.
Any other peace is not only temporary but usually unsatisfying. The
world's definition of peace is the absence of strife and conflict. Jesus
warns us that in this world we will have tribulation. But then He tells us
to cheer up because He has overcome the world! He said that He gives
us His peace and that it is not the kind the world gives.

The peace of God is beautifully illustrated by the story of several
artists who were invited to submit paintings depicting their various
concepts of peace. One painting showed a beautiful mountain meadow,
sheltered by giant trees and flourishing with many flowers of delicate
hue. Another portrayed a quiet stream flowing through a peaceful valley. But the prize-winning painting pictured a steep, rocky cliff, above
which the lightning flashed and the rain beat down in torrents. And in a
small cleft of a rock in the side of the cliff sat a tiny bird, dry and safe,
gazing calmly out at the raging storm. That's what God's peace is: a
safe, quiet place in the midst of the storms of life.

I would have you learn this great fact: that a life of doing right is the wisest life there is. If you live that kind of life, you'll not limp or stumble as you run. Carry out my instructions; don't forget them, for they will lead you to real living.

Proverbs 4:11–13

To those who honor Him and obey His admonitions, God offers a good, long life of riches, honor, pleasure, and peace. What more can we ask?

Denise Gore, an effective, truly successful branch manager who lives in Nashville, Tennessee, found that God could and would give her total fulfillment through these admonitions in Proverbs. Denise is wife of Ed, mother of three teenagers, and manager of over one thousand women. Here is her story:

*Just when we think we know our plan for our lives, God begins to reveal **His** plan—not in one revelation, but piece by piece, as we grow in understanding.*

I was certain that becoming a wife and mother was my total plan for my life. Then a nagging feeling that I could do more and be more kept building inside. God had blessed me with talents, but I was not multiplying all of them. I was cheating. But I had family responsibilities. How could I possibly do more and when? I was confused, and began to search for something. I had always delighted in challenges, particularly if they would cause me to reach beyond what I thought I could do.

Home Interiors and Gifts was an intriguing challenge, but I did not realize it would be my answer.

My whole life then began to have a new direction—achievement, growth, winning, sharing—were added with each new day, each new friend, each goal attained. The excitement and enthusiasm spilled over to my family. They were enriched because an awareness of their needs unfolded in front of me. I wanted to add more to their lives. The fulfillment I had found was also shared with others. The more I gave, the so much more I received! Through Mary, I learned of God's direction for our company, and that each life He created was for success and happiness. Once you belong to God, and commit to follow His plan, He will lead, protect, and support with perfect love.

The more I studied the Book of Proverbs, guided by Mary's wis-

dom, how clearly I perceived God's plan. Simple (but firm) principles which, if followed, lead to the pathway of success for each one. Along with this success is the responsibility to recognize every indi-vidual as God's special child. Learning to lead each one through love, with the confidence that God will guide and strengthen me in His plan, has become a joyful task. I depend completely on this philosophy in my family relationship and all others whom I influence in any way.

Why God has enriched my life is still a wonderment, but my deep commitment to His plan to be the person He wants is my motivation. Growing each day toward that goal is the most exciting journey. The anticipation of what I will be is joy to its fullest measure on earth. That will be my gift multiplied to God.

5

The Things God Loves and the Things God Hates

There are six things the Lord hates—no, seven: Haughtiness, Lying, Murdering, Plotting evil, Eagerness to do wrong, A false witness, Sowing discord among brothers.

Proverbs 6:16–19

Proverbs is specific about the things that God loves and the things that He hates. An essential part of wisdom is realizing what it is that God likes and what He dislikes; then studying ourselves to see if we are doing the things that are pleasing to Him. We have already talked about how God loves the humble, sincere, generous and contrite person. Now let's take a look at the things God says He hates. Let's look at the *entire* list to see if any of these are present in our lives.

Haughtiness. What is haughtiness? Haughtiness is arrogant or egotistical behavior which makes a person look as though he feels superior to others. Haughtiness is trying to put other people down— trying to make ourselves feel and look superior by criticizing others. Sometimes it is nothing more than just a look, or an attitude of smugness.

Strangely enough, the people who are the most guilty of being haughty do not always realize they are behaving in that way. Often they are very insecure and assume a haughty demeanor as a coverup.

Haughtiness is the opposite of a serving nature—it is wanting to *be* served.

It is possible to display an attitude of haughtiness by our lack of patience with the learning process of others. When we communicate by our actions or attitudes ("If you were smarter, you would understand more readily"), even though we don't actually *say* the words, we are nevertheless being haughty. And being haughty is just the opposite of being understanding and loving. It is helpful to remember the "feel, felt, and found" formula: "I understand how you *feel*. I once *felt* that way myself, until I *found* that this plan would make me feel differently about myself—would make me feel successful—would make me be successful."

The second thing Proverbs says God hates is *lying*. Truth is an essential part of life. Once a man's word was considered his bond, and his handshake was his contract. It is sad that we have fallen so far from that ideal. Nowadays even little children frequently receive communication from adults that it is not important to tell the truth.

Perhaps you do not think you are lying when you tell your child to answer the phone and tell someone you are not at home, but your child gets the message. He learns that when it is convenient for him, he can always avoid the truth to escape discomfort. He can learn from you that there is no need for him to discipline himself, or to accept his responsibilities.

Truth is a part of personal integrity. Some time ago, in a seminar for professional and business people from all across the nation, the subject dealt with the "selection, training, and development of tomorrow's executives." After the session ended each person in attendance was asked to write the characteristics that, in his opinion, make a good executive. Everyone agreed that the most important requirement was *personal integrity*.

These people were not preachers or moralists; they were business people who were trying to determine the most essential ingredient in the makeup of a good executive. And *their* unanimous vote was for personal integrity.

Integrity is the foundation for successful living, whether a person is a churchman, a student, a businessman, a homemaker, a husband, or a teenager. Personal integrity can be divided into four parts: moral principles, self-discipline, dependable truthfulness and honesty, and unquestionable honor. Integrity is the cement that holds together all the building blocks of personality, ability, training, talent, and creative genius. Without it there will be cracks in our total makeup, which can very easily cause us to fall apart, can allow any kind of adversity to be our undoing.

The third thing God hates is *murdering*. There is much violence today. In many of our major cities people are afraid to walk the streets at night for fear of being attacked. The violence on our television screen staggers the imagination. We hear of parents even murdering their children and of sons murdering their fathers and mothers. May God have mercy on us!

Jesus said, "Under the laws of Moses the rule was, 'If you kill, you must die.' But I have added to that rule, and tell you that if you are only *angry,* even in your own home, you are in danger of judgment!" (Matthew 5:21, 22).

Who of us can say that our anger never hurts our husband, our children? And if our anger encourages violence on the part of others, it displeases God.

Recently I heard several born-again Christians, who participated with Eldridge Cleaver in the violence of the sixties, tell how they eventually found Christ because Christians had demonstrated love rather than hostility. Even before they saw the light, they respected those who did not become angry. Although they admitted to calling them names at the time, they confessed that they later respected them. We are to be angry about the sin—but still love the sinner.

God hates the *"eagerness to do wrong."* It is true that we all do wrong sometimes, but at times we fall into it and we are not *eager* to do it. However, when people do not have a good value system, they become eager to lie, steal, cheat, or to be promiscuous. Without a good value system, people cannot know how much they really matter to God. They don't realize that they don't have to do wrong things in order to try to prove themselves. People who are not taught the right value system will develop their own system. We must realize that God loves us and that He has a plan for our lives; that doing wrong will only complicate life and thwart God's plan.

> Never forget to be truthful and kind. Hold these virtues tightly. Write them deep within your heart.
>
> Proverbs 3:3

Notice that the writer puts truthfulness and kindliness together. Parents must be truthful and tell children what God expects of them and what His moral absolutes are, showing them the right way with love and kindness. Howard Hendrick's book *Say It With Love* is a great example.

Plotting Evil. Not many people would confess that they might ever be guilty of this wrong, but anytime we gossip, we are plotting evil. Whenever we sow discord (another thing God hates), we are plotting evil.

> . . . This one thing I know: God is for me!
> Psalms 56:9

God is not evil. He hates evil, and if I trust in Him completely, He will help me to stay out of the way of evil.

We pray in the Lord's Prayer, "Lead us not into temptation." God doesn't lead us into the evil way, but we are asking Him in this petition to lead us away from evil. God has promised in His Word that He will keep us from evil, not because of our goodness, but because of His love and His faithfulness. We can have complete confidence, not in ourselves, but in what we can do because our God is faithful. He empowers us. Jesus gets us out of the danger zone of temptation as He did for His disciples in the story in Matthew 14:22.

> Immediately after this, Jesus told his disciples to get into their boat and cross to the other side of the lake while he stayed to get the people started home.

We are to stay close in relationship so we can hear the Holy Spirit of Jesus when He speaks to us.

False Witness. A half-truth is much more dangerous than a lie. One can usually recognize a lie, but a half-truth is more easily believed. Our life today is filled with half-truths, all the way from our history books to our advertising media and our doctrines. We must be on guard.

Sowing discord among your brothers. Gossip is a sin that is just as deadly as alcohol. It destroys a person just as easily, just as completely. We are in the business of building people up, not tearing them down. When someone starts to say something unkind about another, it is well to just stop the conversation and say, "You and I are both intelligent people. I believe we can find something more constructive to talk about."

Perhaps you are now looking at the thing God dislikes most in you, and you may be thinking you just can't be that perfect. You're right! None of us is! Even Paul felt the same way:

. . . my new life tells me to do right, but the old nature that is still inside me loves to sin. Oh, what a terrible predicament I'm in! Who will free me from my slavery to this deadly lower nature? . . .

Romans 7:24, 25

But then Paul goes on: "Thank God! It has been done by Jesus Christ, our Lord. He has set me free."

God does forgive. Christ died on a cruel cross for my sins and for yours. That is the good news that makes us want to change our lives. But God can reward us only if we show by our behavior that we are putting Him first.

Seneca said, "We really believe something when we act as if it were so." If we really believe God—in Him, on Him, and through Him, we will allow Him to make our actions match our beliefs.

Every person must build his or her life around something or someone that does not change. And the only something or someone who does not change is God. He is the only solid rock and all else is but shifting sand. In making Him the hub of the wheel of our existence and in setting goals consistent with His purposes, we find that our spokes are sturdy, our tires are inflated just right, and our journey through life is meaningful and serene.

6

Dreams or Goals?

We should make plans—counting on God to direct us.

Proverbs 16:9

A young mother once called me and told me in detail just how miserable her life was. Her husband constantly criticized her. Her young children would not mind. Life was boring. There was never enough money.

Betty wanted sympathy. But I didn't give her sympathy—not because I didn't feel sorry for her, but rather because I really wanted to help.

"Betty," I asked, "have you set any goals for your life?"

"Goals? Why, of course. I wish we could move out of this apartment into a house with a yard. I would like to have some new clothes. But more than anything else, I want my family to be happy."

"And how do you expect to reach these goals?" I asked.

"Why, I don't know," she replied vaguely. "Those are just . . . 'dreams.' "

How many times had I heard other women express their desires in much the same way! They thought they knew just exactly what they wanted, but they did not know how to get it. *They didn't have goals but only dreams*—fairy-tale wishes requiring a magic wand to turn ugly frogs into princes.

Proverbs doesn't have a magic wand. But it does have advice that will work miracles, if we will but use it.

I would have you learn this great fact: that a life of doing right is the wisest life there is. If you live that kind of life, you'll not

limp or stumble as you run. Carry out my instructions; don't
forget them, for they will lead you to real living.

Proverbs 4:11–13

Real living. Reality. These key words mean that you are not expecting perfection—of yourself or of others. We must all learn to live in
reality. If you would have your dreams come true, you must first figure
out exactly what a life of doing right is—for you. In other words, you
must set your goals.

Yes, God wants you to see your dreams come true. You can open
yourself up to the gift of life and joy that He wants to give to you, if you
are willing to plan and to work for it.

Frances Podboreski had complications with her dislocated hip. She
was always in and out of hospitals. In 1943 doctors told her she would
be in a wheelchair in the near future for the rest of her life. Frances
became our National Queen of Displayers in 1961. I'll always treasure
the opportunity to place a crown on her head and a mink stole around
her shoulders. I've asked Frances to share her feelings:

*1960 was that start of something grand for me. I found Home
Interiors and Pearl Burns and Ruth Shanahan (Mary's daughter) at
my very first Home Interiors Sales Meeting. I have learned to set
goals and make them high, then have a strong determination to
follow through. The challenge, satisfaction, and fulfillment are wonderful. The feeling of accomplishment brings excitement, peace and
contentment within yourself.*

*I am grateful that my Mother began giving me responsibilities
when I was very young. She always gave me courage, love, and
faith. She died suddenly in 1937, but I have always known that she is
by my side. I always tried to do my best, if I was doing something
that I liked, ever since I was very young.*

*Just as Mary says, "People were born and reborn to be victorious.
God never takes time to make a nobody. Be somebody." I love what
I am doing. I love the people I work for. They are my family. I will
never forget the day I met Mary. I never was so excited in my life. I
have said it before and I will say it again, Mary should be President of the United States. Mary, Don, and every woman in the
Home Interiors Staff have given people a new and better vision of
life.*

The best way is to remember that *a goal is the target for your behavior*—then take aim! Aim your behavior right at the bull's eye. If a goal is the target, then to reach that goal you must make your behavior consistent with your goal.

You don't have to change everything all at once. Set your goal. Make a commitment to that goal. Then ask for God's help in achieving it, and let your heart follow.

The only way in which anyone can change his attitudes or his behavior is to work on them, one area at a time.

For example, since Betty wishes for a new house, she can set a goal of making money for a down payment. She can then start aiming her behavior at that goal by doing part-time work. Perhaps she longs for new clothes. If so, she can set a goal of learning how to sew. The wish for a happy family might be met by setting a goal of reading inspirational books, or of obtaining family counseling.

There is little to be gained by falling into the trap of trying to achieve goals by wishing something would happen. That's only dreaming. Ten little words can help you set the right kind of goals:

IF IT IS TO BE, IT IS UP TO ME.

Everything we do every day is either aimed at our goals, or it is not. Many miserable people try doing what feels good at the time, instead of disciplining themselves to work on their behavior. "Feelings" are not reliable. You don't always feel like doing everything that is essential for your happiness and success. You may not "feel" in love with your husband when you are annoyed with him, but you may have to discipline yourself to be understanding and loving, if your goal is a closer relationship.

You may not feel overjoyed when you answer the phone and learn that a friend has a problem and wants to take up precious moments of your time. But if your goal is to serve God by serving others, you will take the time to listen with interest.

If we make a commitment of the will and of the heart to work toward a certain goal, then duty and discipline will carry us through to success.

A word of warning, however: Sometimes dedicated people fail to change their behavior because they have overlooked two important points in the setting of goals:

1. It is important to set realistic goals.
2. Goals must be clearly defined. Goals that are too vague are seldom reached.

Realistic goals. If you set a goal that will be impossible for you to reach, you will automatically fail. Such a failure makes you feel worse about yourself than if you had never tried. I once asked a group of high-school seniors what goals they had set for their lives, and their answers were very revealing.

"I plan to be a lawyer," said the first.

"I'm going to become a master photographer," the second replied.

The third student shrugged realistically. "I just want to pass my exams for now," he admitted. His goal was limited, but for him it was the best goal he could possibly set. He was a borderline student. If he decided to set a realistic goal of passing his exams, he could easily adapt himself to meet the requirements by studying hard. For him to set a goal of trying to be a doctor would have been unrealistic. He did not have the grades in past work which would get him accepted in a college premed course. Such a long-range and ambitious goal would only have frustrated him and destroyed his motivation for trying to pass the senior exams. He would have failed, ending up with a poor attitude about himself.

Goals that are too vague. Betty said she wanted a happy family, but she could not say specifically how she could change her behavior to make herself and her family happier. Her goal was too vague. A more specific goal for Betty might have been to learn to control her tongue, instead of nagging at her family in order that they might be happier.

Many women have idealistic goals of wanting to help others, or to serve God in another way. These are wonderful desires; however, they need to be specific in order to be considered goals. One way might be to start a Bible study in the home. Another might be to do part-time work and earn extra money for a worthwhile cause, or to donate time and services wherever needed. I like the advice written in the margin of an elderly missionary woman's Bible:

> You ask me what is the will of God
> And I will answer true.
> It is the nearest thing that should be done
> That God can do through you.

When dreams come true at last, there is life and joy! We are happier when we are achieving goals than when we are merely waiting and wishing for ugly frogs to turn into princes!

Is it possible to help others make their wishes a reality? How often we see talented people who are failing! We want so badly to help them succeed. But there is really no way we can play fairy godmother. Each person must be *motivated* to reach her own goals. Only then will she be willing to work on the solutions that can overcome obstacles.

We can, however, help people to set their goals. In our Home Interiors organization, new Displayers are encouraged to sit down with their managers before beginning to work and write out their goals for their careers. The Displayer may say, "I want a lot of money." The manager's function is to help the Displayer avoid vagueness.

"How much is a lot?" she asks. Perhaps the new Displayer wants a thousand dollars to help pay for a child's education, or five thousand to make a down payment on a new house. Maybe she wants only three hundred dollars to buy some nice accessories for her home. Whatever the amount is, the manager writes it down on her goal sheet.

If the new Displayer later on fails to reach her goal, the manager can then sit down with her, show her the written goals and say, "Something is wrong. Here are your goals and you are not reaching them." She can help the new Displayer to realize what the problem is and can then suggest ways in which the situation may be remedied. Perhaps the problem is nothing more than the fact that the Displayer has not been attending sales meetings regularly, and is thus depriving herself of a good source of training and motivation. With a little encouragement in this area, the Displayer can begin to reach her goal.

It is possible to help, however, *only* if help is wanted. If it is not, we can pray about the attitude and behavior of the person in question. I've found that the best thing I can do to help someone else is to work on my own behavior.

Sometimes it is possible to create in a person a desire to change by helping that person achieve a better self-image. I once visited the young, frightened girls who were in a home for unwed mothers. Many of them could have been attractive, but, due to their poor attitudes about themselves, they did nothing to improve their straggly hair, sloppy attire, and bad complexions. It did little good for me to try to tell them they could be pretty. Without self-esteem, they could not imagine themselves as being attractive.

One day I took some Home Interiors plaques, figurines, and candles to the home. I permitted each girl to choose something for her own room. The girls were thrilled. I used this happy time to talk to them about how they could make their rooms more attractive places in which to live. As the girls started caring about their rooms, they also became eager to talk about making themselves pretty. And as they began to work at improving their appearance, other areas of behavior changed for the better.

Every person wants to believe that his life counts for something. How wonderful that it is possible to make our lives count with the aid of our Source Book, the Bible! In it God has provided just what we need.

Many people have not been taught to have goals. Many live dull, humdrum existences. Because they have never been encouraged to have dreams, they feel life is meaningless. They have never learned the secret of turning their wishes into realistic and attainable goals by simply changing their attitudes and their behavior—one step at a time!

Think big! Attempt great things.
Believe big! And you'll get big results.
Don't sweat the small stuff.

Proverbs tells us that a life of doing right is the wisest life there is. If we set goals and commit ourselves to achieving them, then ask God to bless our efforts, we can make our dreams and wishes come true!

Let me share an experience with you that illustrates the practical application of these truths.

Bonnie Kelley is a personal "recruit" and friend of mine. She was a registered nurse when I first met her. She was not actively pursuing her profession, for she wanted to be mother to two children, wife to her husband, Troy, and still be an individual with time for herself; yet, her self-image was very low at the time. Here, let Bonnie tell you herself. (Bonnie is now a leading branch manager with confidence.)

Yes, it brings back a warmth to my thoughts to recall the first time I met Mary Crowley. There was a special glow that she transmitted to me.

As a registered nurse, I'd never considered making a career change. But when I attended a meeting and Mrs. Crowley shared tips on personal development and fulfillment, I found myself enjoying the possibility of such growth. My self-esteem was low; but Mrs. Crowley saw me as a winner and transmitted her confidence to me.

She believed there was potential for me. She saw the best, expected the best, and it caused me to respond.

Under the guiding hand of her training, it has enabled me to succeed in all areas of my life. It has been my privilege to speak at universities, and before other large audiences including Rotary and Optimist meetings. My service to my community has grown, in such activities as heading up YMCA membership drives, being on a hospital board, teaching adult Sunday-school classes, and others.

Where does all of this great training come from? At a good many of our training sessions we have been taught from Proverbs; taught that true wisdom comes from God. How to use common sense and the value of hard work is stressed. Many people search for the secrets of life. The greatest purest nuggets for life and success can be found in Proverbs.

The greatest training has been from the examples set before me. Yes, all because two people, my husband, Troy, and Mary Crowley, saw me as a winner—and believed.

7

How to Set Goals

To learn, you must want to be taught . . . .
Proverbs 12:1

Do you believe in praying for what you want?

God desires to give us many good things. The Bible tells us that. But God does not grant the things we ask Him for unless our every attitude indicates to Him that we are really desirous of the things for which we ask. God will care just as much as we care about our goals and desires. If we are not actively participating with God to make possible the things we desire, we are merely dreaming. If we are not actively setting goals and working toward them, we are only wishing.

When a football player wants to make the team, but does not discipline himself by practicing and by learning the plays, we conclude that he really doesn't have a burning desire to make the first-string. He may want to play football, but unless he is motivated to do what is required to make the team, success will elude him.

If, on the other hand, the athlete works hard, eats properly, keeps training rules and memorizes the plays the coach assigns, his behavior verifies his real desire to be a first-string player. It is likely that as he prays to achieve his goal, God will honor his prayers and success will follow.

> Have two goals: wisdom—that is, knowing and doing right—
> and common sense. Don't let them slip away, for they fill you
> with living energy, and are a feather in your cap.
> *Proverbs 3:21, 22*

We can learn to know what is right by studying the Bible and by attending worship. We can learn to do right by setting goals to change our behavior—and by leaning on God's strength. If we learn to practice this kind of wisdom, then Proverbs promises abundant energy, which will help us accomplish more than we ever believed possible.

Bill Gothard, well-known Christian educator and lecturer, and founder of the Institute in Basic Youth Conflicts, says that there are seven areas of life in which it is important for us to set goals: *intellectual, emotional, physical, spiritual, social, family,* and *financial.* As a career woman, I have added to that list the area of *business-career.* This vital area affects or is affected by all the others.

On page 49 is a chart which has proved helpful to many. I suggest that you take the time to fill it in and then refer to it frequently. I think you will find that it will be helpful to you, too!

What you write on *your* chart will be entirely different from what I would write on mine. Setting goals is a highly individual matter. Each of us has different problems, needs, and desires, as well as different tastes.

It is important, however, for you to consider each goal carefully. After doing so, write down your thoughts as to what your goals should be and what the possible obstacles might be to reaching each goal. Finally, write down the possible solutions to each obstacle. In the TIME FRAME column, write down a date when you expect to begin working on each goal (as well as a date when you want to attain it). Check your progress weekly and note your findings in the PROGRESS REPORT column. Don't forget to include in the POSSIBLE REWARDS column the benefits you will receive from attaining each goal. To stimulate thinking about how to fill in your goal sheet, let's look at each of the areas to be considered.

Intellectual goals. Perhaps you might wish to begin reading some inspirational books or study information necessary for your job. If so, write it down under possible goals. The possible obstacles might be that you are a slow reader, or that you have vision problems. Perhaps you have little or no time for reading. As possible solutions, you might use cassettes instead of books. Perhaps you need new glasses. You could set aside some time each day for reading. The possible rewards are that you may become a more interesting, fulfilled person, or one who is more knowledgeable on the job.

HAPPINESS IS ACHIEVING WORTHWHILE GOALS

Mary C. Crowley

Area of Life	Possible Goals	Possible Obstacles	Possible Solutions	Time Frame	Possible Rewards	Progress Report
INTELLECTUAL						
EMOTIONAL						
PHYSICAL						
SPIRITUAL						
SOCIAL						
FAMILY						
FINANCIAL						
BUSINESS-CAREER						

"A GOAL IS THE TARGET OF YOUR BEHAVIOR."

Emotional goals. You might want to heighten your appreciation of your loved ones, or of the beauty around you. A recovered alcoholic once told me that he had never been able to fully realize the loveliness of his wife, his home, his children—even his yard. Each time he had taken a drink, his awareness of the beauty that should have stirred his emotions was dulled. Drugs, too, can dull awareness. But so can the fact that you are too busy to notice—or too tired—or too worried.

One of the greatest enemies of womankind is fatigue. It clouds our decisions and erodes our dispositions. Everything looks different to us when we are rested and refreshed.

A word about worry. Worry is the biggest waste in the world. It accomplishes exactly nothing. Worry never robs tomorrow of its sorrow. It only saps today of its strength.

If either of these conditions is an obstacle for you, the solution might be to become more organized, or to use your time more efficiently. And if you find that resentments and irritations are taking the place of gratitude and appreciation in your life, you might find it helpful to start thanking God each day for the source of the irritation: your husband, your home, your children, the family automobile. The possible rewards are greater happiness for you and for others as you find your own attitudes changing to those of gratitude and appreciation.

Physical goals. Perhaps you would like to lose weight and the big obstacle is food, or having to cook for your family, or having to eat out as you travel to work. There are many possible solutions: You might change the eating habits of your family; resist buying snack foods; start reading books on nutrition; learn about food supplements and salt substitutes. Start eating a breakfast heavy in protein. I have to plan a period of fifteen minutes of stretching and breathing exercises every day. It takes discipline! Of course, our main goal should be glowing good health! You'll find the rewards will be obvious in your mirror!

Spiritual goals. Do you long to know God better? to have more time to spend with Him? to have such a strong relationship to Jesus Christ that you feel Him working in your life and overcoming the character defects that you recognize in yourself? If so, set a goal to intensify your relationship with God.

The possible obstacles may be that you are just too busy, or perhaps you are concerned that if you insist on having a prayer time every morning, your family will think you are a fanatic. Perhaps you are afraid that you will lose friends. The possible solutions are to spend more time with other Christians so that your behavior will not be adversely influenced by non-Christians. Read your Bible daily. Join a Bible-study group, or start one. Pray every morning and learn to re-place doubt and frustration with faith and prayers.

What are the possible rewards of enhancing your spiritual life? You will be blessed. You'll have a victorious life and be better able to function. You will be filled with more energy, and you'll be calmer and more serene, even on the more trying days!

Social goals. All of us need friends, but friends don't just happen. We have to cultivate relationships. In doing this, you might decide that you are going to be more sensitive to the needs of the other people you know. More specifically, you might find that you will want to express your gratitude to the people who regularly perform essential services for you—services that are normally taken for granted. I have found that a small gift and a personal note of recognition and thanks mean a great deal to the people who do important things for me, such as taking away my trash, and it always inspires them to do a better job.

The obstacles to your social goals may be many. Maybe you are just too busy to take the time to think of others. Possibly you just do not see people such as waitresses and busboys as real people with real con-cerns and needs. Perhaps your mind is on other things, or you are too shy to reach out to others.

The solutions might be to begin by doing simple, thoughtful things such as writing little notes to people who don't get much mail. The rewards? You will have more friends and you'll have the satisfaction of bringing joy to others.

Family goals. We all want to have a close, happy family. Perhaps your goal in this area might be to learn to have more patience with others. You might also improve the quality of your time together by having family devotions.

The possible obstacles might be that you find it hard to get the whole family together at one time, because everyone is busy and on a differ-ent schedule. Perhaps there is not enough time. Possible solutions could be to watch less television or to otherwise utilize your time better. You might make a trip to the supermarket do double duty by taking one of your children with you and giving that child your undi-vided attention for a time. And on the rare moments when you are alone with your husband, pay attention to him and let him know that he is loved and appreciated. The rewards will be greater happiness for your entire family.

Financial goals. You may want to have a better house—to be free of debt—to contribute to the Lord's work. The possible obstacles to these goals might be your recklessness with charge accounts. If you are unable to use credit wisely and with restraint, a good solution might be to destroy them and start paying cash. You will be rewarded with peace of mind, as you will find yourself getting free of debt. Remember that the most uncomfortable place to live is just beyond your income!

Business goals. If all your goals are worthwhile and are being met satisfactorily, you are likely to find that you are achieving your goals in business, providing they are worthy, specific, timely, and realistic.

> Wisdom is the main pursuit of sensible men, but a fool's goals are at the ends of the earth!
>
> Proverbs 17:24

Wisdom is a necessary factor in the selection of prudent goals, and God has promised to give wisdom. The Bible tells us that He will give wisdom liberally to those who ask for it. What a wonderful thing to know that we can have the wisdom from above, just for the asking!

As we seek the wisdom of God when we set specific and attainable goals, as we gradually conform ourselves to God's pattern for our lives and start chipping away at the barriers that stand between ourselves and what we desire to achieve with God's help, we are amazed to find that our lives have begun to change in dramatic ways. We become more productive, more successful, happier. It seems that we can see miracles being wrought right before our eyes!

But God is in the miracle business, and we are co-laborers with Him. As we seek to apply His heavenly principles to our lives, we cannot help but be successful!

Mary Crowley and managers at White House. *Right to left*: Nancy Good, Donna Mauricio, Mary Lou Mickey, Pat O'Connor, Shelley Randolph, Mary C, Pearl Burns, Peggy Foster. *Below:* Rosalynn Carter, Owen Cooper, Mary C, President Carter. Official photograph, The White House, 2 May 1978.

Mary C with Gerald Ford.
Bob Kornegay Photography,
Dallas, Texas. *Left:* Mary C
and Billy Graham.

Mary C with Pat Boone at 1973 Dallas Seminar. Bob Kornegay Photography. *Left:* Dave and Mary C. Bob Kornegay Photography.

Don Carter (son) and Mary C. Twentieth Anniversary celebration. Bob Kornegay Photography. *Below:* Daughter Ruth and Mary C. Bob Kornegay Photography.

Mary C with Bob Hope. Twentieth Anniversary Seminar. *Below:* Donna Mauricio, a real winner. Bob Kornegay Photography.

Winner! Pearl Burns. Bob Kornegay Photography. *Below:* National Queen Betty Byrum and Mary C, 1977 Seminar. Bob Kornegay Photography.

Denise Gore, Nashville, Tenn. Bob Kornegay Photography. *Below:* Don Carter, Frances Podboreski (our Second National Queen), Pearl Burns, Mary C, 1976 seminar, Philadelphia. Bob Kornegay Photography.

Mary C and managers: Reba Kornegay, Trish Baird, Linda Currey, Pat Anderson, Bonnie Kelley. *Below:* Barbara Hammond, Mary C. and Peaches Mathews. Bob Kornegay Photography.

Mary C and two winners.
Bob Kornegay Photography.
Below: Carol Lawrence
with Mary Crowley and
Nanci Hammond. Bob Kor-
negay Photography.

8

Heaven Help the Home!

Commit your work to the Lord, then it will succeed.

Proverbs 16:3

It is better to live in a corner of an attic than in a beautiful home with a cranky, quarrelsome woman.

Proverbs 25:24

Love has a locale here on earth and it is called the home. Home is where love is nourished, where it is best expressed. Out of the home all other relationships are influenced.

The home is the place where character is formed. In Home Interiors we feel the home should be a haven—a place of refuge, peace, harmony, and beauty. We encourage our people to develop attraction power in the home. Not only are we speaking of beautiful accessories and attractive colors but—more importantly—the attractiveness of the people who live there.

My good friend, Howard Hendricks, renowned lecturer on the home, often says, "Heaven help the home!" The woman, he maintains, must be the magnet in the home "to draw the husband home at the close of day and children home at the close of play." Each home needs that kind of magnetism if it is to provide the necessary warmth and stability for all its members.

It is true that many women work outside the home, either part-time or full-time. They come home at the end of the day and still have lots of work awaiting them there. Many advocates for Women's Lib are saying that it is just impossible for a working woman to make the effort that is required to create a loving atmosphere in the home.

Many women have discovered, however, that a loving atmosphere does not depend on the amount of time involved, but rather on the depth of the commitment to the family structure.

It is better to live in a corner of an attic than in a beautiful house with a cranky, quarrelsome woman.

Proverbs 25:24

In the marriage ceremony, couples pledge to love each other " 'til death us do part.'' And all too often the death that occurs is the death of the relationship rather than an actual physical death. How easy it is for today's beautiful bride to become tomorrow's nagging wife—unless she has a commitment.

Many things in life tend to tarnish and must be polished frequently in order to stay new and shiny. Love, too, needs to be constantly shined and polished, protected and nourished, lest it grow dim and lose its lustre.

It is difficult to build a strong family life for Satan's greatest attacks today are on the home. To quote Edith Schaeffer, wife of Dr. Francis Schaeffer of L'Abri, "We are endeavoring to preserve an endangered species—the family!''

It is not impossible, however, to build a good home. *The first prerequisite is a right relationship with God,* for our relationship with our Heavenly Father directly affects all others. This relationship, above all, must be genuine and vital, for nothing grieves our Father more than when we merely go through the motions. He wants to be real to us.

Jesus said, "The Father and I are one." He spent time with His Father in a close personal relationship, always drawing aside and seeking communion with God. We need that personal, individual time to commune with our Father, just as Jesus did, and we must follow our Savior's example.

Our second priority of commitment is to our husbands. Strange, that after children come they so often grab first place, then grow up and go away leaving two strangers who—thanks to those children—no longer know each other! The husband-wife commitment must always supersede that of commitment to the children. If this is not the case, nobody will be secure—not even the children.

I recall a beloved pastor who once felt his ministry was even more important than his family. The day his first child was born, a church member telephoned with what purported to be an emergency. The pastor left his wife on her very first night home with a new baby, only to discover that there really was not an emergency after all. The pastor said it took a long time for the hurt of that experience to heal in his wife. It was, however, through this misfortune that he learned a valuable lesson: that his responsibility to his family was second only to his obligation to God. Not even his *ministry* came ahead of it.

Let's look again at your relationship with your husband. Do you remember when you were first married—how shopping, cooking, and housekeeping seemed such fun? Then, after a time, housework became routine and nobody even seemed to notice it unless you didn't do it. At last it became almost drudgery.

The routine aspects of an activity can soon rob it of its joy. God instilled in every human being the hunger for stimulation, excitement, and romance. That's why He created the world in color! He could have made it in black and white, and it would have functioned just as well, but God knew that this aesthetic creature called man would need color and beauty to inspire and excite him. What wonderful things God has given us for pure enjoyment!

Today when man cuts down the trees and plows up the grass and sows concrete and asphalt in their place, we must work harder to bring the extra color, romance, and beauty into our lives.

Sometimes, after several years of marriage, a woman will say, "Well, I just don't love him any more." William James of Harvard University, the most famous psychologist in America at the turn of the century, used to say, "It is easier to act your way into feeling, than to feel your way into acting."

When love fades, it is always because actions are following feelings and it should be the other way around. So if you don't feel love any more, *act as if you did*. Behave as you did on your honeymoon, as you did on the first day of marriage, or even when you were dating. And if you keep on *acting as if,* the feeling of love will return!

Love is much more than mere feeling. It is commitment. It is necessary for us to have a real commitment to marriage, home, the job—even if we don't feel like it at times. It is a fact of life that most of the work in the world is done by people who do not "feel" like it. If we keep on doing the things that make marriage work and stop worrying about our feelings, we will soon be surprised and happy to realize that, somewhere along the way, we began to feel like it!

Often we make the mistake of thinking that we can change our husbands, but we must remember that only God can change people. It is our job to make our husbands happy, and God's job to make them good. Remember, when you took your wedding vows you said, "I do,"—not "I will *re-do*." As Billy Graham's lovely wife, Ruth says, "Don't marry a man you are not willing to adjust to." If, however, you are already married, as most of us are, then be willing to adjust. After all, why should he do all the adjusting?

Third on the list of priorities *is our relationship with our children*. The successful parent works himself out of the job, but never out of the relationship. Remember that the kindest thing you can ever do for your children is to teach them to be independent of you—but dependent on the Lord.

One of the best gifts we can ever give our children is our time. We must be sensitive to their need for our time and attention, and we must aid them in building self-confidence and in developing a good self-image. When our school system teaches the Theory of Evolution as fact, and our children hear that they are descended from primates, how can they possibly have a good self-image? How different they become when they learn that they are indeed created in God's image and likeness! How wonderful for them to know that they are special, that God has a plan for their lives! It is so vital that every boy and girl feel like somebody—and *be* somebody!

Fourth on the list of commitments is *our relationship with special people* or, as Morris Shieks calls them, "the significant others." These would be the people, relatives and friends, who are special in your life. My grandmother always urged me to expose my children to exciting, attractive Christian adults outside the family. Most children do not always listen to the members of their own family, and they need someone else to keep them balanced. They need role models outside the family to emulate.

And finally is our commitment to everyone else with whom we are involved in daily living. These are the people whom Jesus referred to when He told us to love our neighbor as ourselves. It is interesting that Jesus suggested here that we definitely are supposed to love ourselves. And loving ourselves means nothing more than having a good self-image, *liking* and *respecting* ourselves. If we do not first love ourselves, then we can never be free of ourselves.

Unfortunately, not all women love themselves. Many do not have a good self-image and do not feel like winners. Many tend to think of themselves only as extensions of their husbands, and not as separate individuals.

Every woman is a "somebody," and she needs to think of herself as a distinct individual and not just as her husband's wife. Others, too, will then think of her in that way. Deborah in the Book of Judges in the Bible, the great heroine of the Israelites, was the wife of a man named Lappidoth. She was not called Mrs. Lappidoth, however; she was known as the mother of Israel!

Remember, to God *you* are a person. God knows your name and He never mistakes you in a crowd! If God thinks of you as a special individual, don't you think you should be one?

Heaven help the home! May God protect the home from all the enemies that assail it—from without and from within. The threats to the home from outside are great, but the ones that attack it from within are just as deadly.

> Take us the foxes, the little foxes that spoil the vines: for our vines have tender grapes.
>
> Song of Solomon 2:15 KJV

Little foxes. Petty persistent irritations. Little problems that nibble away destructively at the very foundation of the home. Like termites, small but deadly, they destroy from within. Harriet Beecher Stowe described very aptly this area of vulnerability in family relationships:

> *You may build beautiful, convenient, attractive houses. You may hang the walls with lovely pictures and stud them with gems of art. There may be living there together persons bound by blood and affection in one common interest, leading a life common to themselves, apart from others. And these persons may each of them be possessed of good and noble traits. There may be a common base of affection, of generosity, of good principles of religion. And yes, through the influence of these perverse, nibbling, insignificant little foxes, half the clusters of happiness of these so promising vines may fail to come to maturity.*
>
> *Yes, the home may hold a little community of people, all of whom may be willing to die for each other. And yet they cannot live happily together, or they achieve far less happiness than their circumstances and fine traits entitle them to expect.*

The reason? Home is the place not only of strong affections, but of entire abandon. It is "undress rehearsal"—the back room—the dressing room from which we go forth to more careful and guarded relationships, leaving behind us much debris of cast-off, everyday clothing.

May God help us to make our homes a refuge—a place of peace, harmony, and beauty—a place where love is expressed. Expressed in tasteful decorations, in clean and cared-for clothing and in attractive meals. But even more, let it be expressed in caring, in supporting one another, in prayer for one another. Let the result be the strengthening of family ties which will make it impossible for the little foxes of inconsideration and irritation to spoil the vines of domestic tranquility.

As we sanctify ourselves, first to God, then to our families, and finally to others, we build and strengthen the bonds of all these various relationships. In so doing, we prepare ourselves and others for the task of reaching out in ministry to a cold and hurting world.

9

Husbands Are for Loving

When a man is gloomy, everything seems to go wrong; when he is cheerful, everything seems right!

Proverbs 15:15

The lady on the other end of the telephone tearfully sobbed out the announcement that she was thinking of getting a divorce. If her husband really loved her, he wouldn't act that way, she insisted. He wouldn't be so hateful.

"What does he do that is so bad?" I asked her gently.

A short pause followed. At last she replied, "Oh, I don't *know*. He's not really mean or anything. It's just that he . . . gets on my *nerves!*"

He gets on her nerves. Amazing! Very patiently I explained to her that I don't know of any man who would not get on a woman's nerves at some time during their marriage, and that it certainly was not grounds for breaking up a home. I reminded her that in any marriage there are days when the wife is ready to give her husband an Oscar for Best Mate of the Year—and other days when she could cheerfully choke him! Who ever said that marriage is all romance and glitter? And who expects it? The only thing that makes marriage work is commitment—and not emotion. The Book of Proverbs contains some excellent advice for helping marriages to be successful.

Hatred stirs old quarrels, but love overlooks insults.

Proverbs 10:12

The fool who provokes his family to anger and resentment will finally have nothing worthwhile left . . . .

Proverbs 11:29

Pride leads to arguments; be humble, take advice and become wise.

Proverbs 13:10

When applied to marriage these Proverbs tell us that we should avoid hatred and resentment that can provoke our husbands, and that we should beware of pride that gets in our way when we should forgive. Other Proverbs tell us the kind of behavior we should practice:

A soft answer turns away wrath, but harsh words cause quarrels.

Proverbs 15:1

Gentle words cause life and health; griping brings discouragement.

Proverbs 15:4

Kind and gentle words have saved many a marriage. But it's also true that sometimes you just don't feel like overlooking the things your husband does. You feel you have a right to become angry.

But wait! Is there really any way you can force your husband to change his behavior? You may get your own way by applying pressure, as only a woman can, but what will it profit you if it generates resentment in your husband? Have you considered the possibility of helping the situation by changing your own behavior? If you are being assertive with your husband, you may be saying the very things that destroy his motivation and cause him to not want to please you.

A worthy wife is her husband's joy and crown; the other kind corrodes his strength and tears down everything he does.

Proverbs 12:4

Sometimes you have to pay the most attention to your husband when you don't think it is necessary, but this is your responsibility as a wife. If your desire is to enrich your marriage, then you will make the effort. The chances are very likely that you will reap exactly what you sow. Make a goal of the commitment of your will and your mind to strengthening your marriage and you will be happy to find that your heart and your emotions will fall right in line.

> Love forgets mistakes . . . .
>
> Proverbs 17:9

Do you ever make any mistakes? Are you willing to forgive yourself and forget them? Be as eager to forget his mistakes as you are to forget your own! Learn to forgive—and forget! Remember that when God forgives your sins, He blots them out. The Bible says He remembers them no more. Real forgiving is forgetting.

And you don't have to be a drudgy doormat, either. One of the best ways in which you can build up your husband is to be a wife he can be proud of. Look your best at all times and don't neglect your appearance. Men like pretty women. Do yourself—and your husband—a favor and invest in a few clothes that will make you look attractive and feel good. Don't be a martyr, always sacrificing for the kids. If somebody has to settle for second best, let it be the kids. Never mind the fact that someone may criticize you for doing that. What do you want most—their approval, or the admiration of your husband? Don't be one of those women who sacrifices for years to give her children everything, and then ends up feeling hurt because they are ashamed of the way she looks. There is something in human nature that looks at every woman as either a doormat or a goddess. You owe it to your husband and to yourself—and even to your kids—to be a goddess.

> A beautiful woman lacking discretion and modesty is like a fine gold ring in a pig's snout.
>
> Proverbs 11:22

That means don't be ridiculous in your effort to be attractive. Don't become self-centered to the point of self-consciousness, and end up behaving like a teenage flirt. Be a lady and not a femme fatale. Use discretion. There is more to being attractive than just looking good.

Be sensitive to your husband's feelings. Remember, men have feelings too, even though in our society they are trained not to let them show. Don't rush ahead and start telling him about the exciting (or terrible) day you've had before even inquiring about his day.

And don't ever make him uncomfortable about his earning capacity. If you have a career, you may possibly earn more money than your husband, as is frequently true among women in Home Interiors. This can be a real threat, unless it is handled sensibly and tactfully. You

must learn quickly to think of your income as "ours" and not "mine."
You may wish to have a bank account of your own for the purpose of
establishing your own credit in the event you should ever need it. A
smart thing to do would be not to put all of your money in your separate
account, but to have the bulk of your combined assets in a joint account. Marriage means share and share alike, because what affects one
person in marriage always affects the other.

At Home Interiors we believe in giving God the glory, knowing that
it is not because *we* are so terrific that we are prosperous, but that our
success is God's gift, and without His help we would have nothing. The
Lord's blessing is our greatest wealth.

Another problem in marriage is that a woman requires more demon-
stration of love than the husband is usually prepared to give. Most men
are usually not aware of the great need that women have for demon-
stration of their affection—women need reassurance. Sometimes, too,
a man will show affection but it won't be in the way that his wife wishes
he would. She may be thinking "breakfast in bed," and he's just thinking *bed*. Perhaps she is thinking "get out the vacuum cleaner and help
me," and he's thinking "help her by getting out of her way for a
while." Maybe she would like dinner out, and his thoughts are running
to sending out for a pizza and watching the game.

I used to have a real problem with feeling neglected because my
husband didn't buy me Christmas or birthday gifts. He was just never
taught that he was supposed to do that. Every Christmas I would have
to psych myself up by concentrating on all his good points, and telling
myself that gifts don't matter (even though I do love to give them).

One Christmas Dave got the urge to give me a belated gift. He
backed my car onto the front lawn (before I realized what was going
on) and washed it for me. When I looked out the window all I could see
was two ugly ruts in our pretty grass—scars that would last through the
winter. I quickly reminded myself that he *had* washed the car out of
love for me, and I smiled and thanked him, keeping quiet about the
ruts. And I kept on keeping quiet when we later discovered that the
weight of the car had broken a gas pipe buried beneath the lawn, and
that repair would cost fifty dollars. *Of course,* there are things that I
would like to have had for Christmas more than I wanted a new gas
pipe under the ground. But you don't think I told him that, do you? Not
on your life!

The best gifts are the ones that cannot be bought. For example, Dave
wears a happy-face pin on one lapel and my picture on the other lapel.

Sometimes he tells our friends, "This is who makes me happy," show-ing my picture. "And that is how happy she makes me." (Showing the happy man!)

> For God loved the world so much that he gave his only Son so that anyone who believes in him shall not perish but have eternal life.
>
> John 3:16

This is a good verse to remember always, but particularly when you're feeling unloved. We are only human, and although we want and need love, none of us is capable of giving the perfect love that God gives. Since we are so important to God that He sent His Son to die for us, why should we require constant reassurance from anyone else that we are loved?

God's love gives us a special kind of security and fulfillment. One of the greatest blessings of knowing Him is that we are so fulfilled that we do not then have to expect so much of anyone else. At the same time, we are so blessed that we are able to give more. In giving more and expecting less, we find the key that unlocks the door, so that we begin to receive in abundance the human love that we had longed for!

Another way in which we can begin to receive more love is to learn to give what is needed. Too often we think only of giving what *we* want to give, instead of thinking of what the other person wants. That is not a gift; it is self-indulgence. Suppose that in your desire to do something extra special for your husband you decide to spend his day off in the kitchen baking him a pie. Well, that's great—except maybe what he would really like is a few stolen moments alone with you. What do you think bakeries are for?

Marriage is largely a matter of give and take, and we must be sure that we are not taking more than we are giving. We need to become sensitive to what is needed, and then we need to learn how to give it graciously, from the heart. Sometimes we just need to give in, although we know that we are in the right and the other person should be the one to give in. Who cares? Give in anyway. Remember that it is possible to win the battle and still lose the war. That's not so smart. We need to learn to be good givers—and good *for*givers!

We need to keep on keeping on—even when we don't feel like it. Jesus called it "going the second mile." Since He commanded us to do it, we can be sure that He will provide the will and the strength. And the reward.

We wives need to concentrate on being less critical. Go easy on the complaints and heavy on the compliments. There should be at least ten compliments for every complaint. Find something every day to praise your husband for. You'll be surprised to find how quickly it will start paying off. Work at changing yourself instead of trying to change your husband. Get off his back. You'll see great changes in him, as he sees you trying to be the kind of wife he'd like you to be.

The Bible tells us to speak in truth, in love, and we need to remember that the law of love is higher than that of honesty. The truth without love can be damaging. In dealing with those we love, it is always necessary to make a deposit of love before we can make a withdrawal of criticism. Otherwise we may suddenly find that we have bankrupted ourselves.

> Yes, if you want better insight and discernment, and are searching for them as you would for lost money or hidden treasure, then wisdom will be given you, and knowledge of God himself; you will soon learn the importance of reverence for the Lord and of trusting him.
>
> Proverbs 2:3–5

Seek God's wisdom in learning to make marriage work by seeing things from your husband's viewpoint instead of your own. God, who is all-loving and all-wise, knows exactly how to impart to us His love and His wisdom to be used in and out of marriage—for the greater joy of those we love, for our own personal enrichment and joy, and for His greater glory!

10

The Forces That Control Our Society

We can make our plans, but the final outcome is in God's hands.

Proverbs 16:1

Scientists spend much time studying the earth, space, and the celestial bodies in order to discover how we human beings fit into the grand scheme of things. So involved are they with their various intellectual approaches, that they usually fail to be aware of the real wisdom that comes from God's marvelous Book—the Bible.

It is vital for us to realize that the only way we will ever be able to build lasting relationships with our children is to know God and to teach them His precepts. The Book of Proverbs tells us we have a choice to make.

> Listen to my counsel—oh, don't refuse it—and be wise. Happy is the man who is so anxious to be with me that he watches for me daily at my gates, or waits for me outside my home! For whoever finds me finds life and wins approval from the Lord. But the one who misses me has injured himself irreparably. Those who refuse me show that they love death.
>
> Proverbs 8:33–36

The Old Testament tells us to teach God's love to our children when they get up and when they go to bed, to write it on their foreheads,

write it on their hearts, write it on the doorposts. It is a grave responsibility to rear children so that they will choose God's wisdom rather
than the path to destruction.

A mother's job today is much harder than it was in Old Testament
days. Society now is subtly controlled by many influences in the home,
school, media, church, government, and, in addition, the sports and
entertainment world. Unfortunately, the effect is often negative rather
than constructive.

Home. Many families have simply abdicated their responsibility to
teach their children to depend on God and the Bible for help in decision
making. Most are too busy for family prayer or for attending church.
Worship and Bible study have been replaced by television and other
activities. We must realize that when we fail to train and instruct our
children properly in the home, we are leaving them wide open to evil
influences.

School. Our public schools are instructing our children in the ways of
socialism and humanism. Prayer and Bible teaching are prohibited.
Science teachers are telling children that man evolved from animal life
rather than that he was created by God, in God's image.

Sex education is popular in schools, but there is little or no emphasis
on morality. An attitude of permissiveness prevails. Despite the sex
education, illegitimacy and disease among teenagers is on the rise. In
addition, our children are being given the idea that they have a right to
be cared for from the cradle to the grave. Young people are being given
too many rights and not enough of a sense of responsibility.

The media. Violence and sex fill our newspapers and our television
programs. You may think you can watch or read anything you wish and
it won't affect you, if you are a Christian, but this is not true. The mind
is like a garden. What you plant is what you harvest. When the seeds of
righteousness are planted, a crop of right values is the result.

The Church. Worship is essential, and it is difficult to imagine how any
church can exert a negative influence. But that is exactly what happens
when a church is so busy taking stands on social issues that the Word of
God and the worship of God are forgotten. The right church will encourage people to enjoy their relationship to God and with one another.
I am especially thankful for the fact that in my own First Baptist

Church of Dallas, the Gospel is preached and the love of God is shared. Find a Bible-preaching church where the fellowship cares about one another—both are equally important.

Government. A democracy is the highest form of government. But our democracy is filtered down through hundreds of bureaucracies and agencies that appear to have as their sole purpose the whittling away of our children's independence and incentive. Waste is encouraged! The system is dulling the God-given desire to work that has built this nation. The men who head these bureaus are appointed rather than elected. They spend our tax money unwisely and are not responsible to anyone. Since we didn't vote them in, we can't vote them out. Many of our congressmen regularly travel the cocktail circuit, and often pass legislation while under the influence of alcohol.

There is much waste. A recent article in the Denver *Post* quoted the Department of Agriculture as stating that no child who is served a free public-school lunch may receive a second glass of milk, unless he is served an entire school meal. Consequently, the child drinks the milk but throws away the food because he cannot eat it. Common sense would indicate that it is less expensive to give the milk alone and better for the child not to waste food.

> A lazy fellow has trouble all through life; the good man's path
> is easy!
>
> Proverbs 15:19

Our government is teaching our children laziness that will handicap them all their lives. How important it is for us to be aware of how our government works and to seek to better it in every way possible. This is one of the goals at Home Interiors.

Our nation was built on the principle of lifting people up—now the government seems to be trying to level everybody out!

Sports and entertainment. How many movie and television stars have died from drug overdose? Many prominent people flout moral laws yet are rich, successful, and famous. Unfortunately a great deal of irresponsible behavior goes on in the world of sports and entertainment, where it is observed by children.

Our young people need heroes after whom they can model themselves. I am so thankful for the Fellowship of Christian Athletes—a wonderful organization, whose purpose is to help young people find the joys of the Christian life. There are plenty of heroes in the world of the FCA and I especially thank the Lord for Coach Tom Landry and Roger Staubach.

Several years ago, when Dave and I were invited on the set of *Green Acres* as Tom Lester's guests, we had to be cleared by the guard at the front gate. When we told him that we were Tom's friends, he smiled enthusiastically. ''Not every person here subscribes to what Tom believes,'' he said, ''but he has certainly made a mark on this set.''

Later, Zsa Zsa Gabor added in her tinkling accent, ''People thought that when Tom came here he would change—but Tommy not change!'' Others in the entertainment world, such as Pat Boone, Dean Jones, and Tom Lester, also stand for God in a beautiful way.

God's Word promises many wonderful things for His people and His promises are not foreshortened. They will be fulfilled. I can see much prophecy being fulfilled even in my lifetime. Back during World War II when Hitler was stuffing his gas ovens with the bodies of Jews, I remember reading Bible passages that promised a return of the Jews to the Promised Land. At that time it seemed impossible that the Jews, persecuted by Hitler and scattered over the earth, would ever return to Judah. Now we see how the land of Israel has been built up in just a few years.

> If my people will humble themselves and pray, and search for me, and turn from their wicked ways, I will hear them from heaven and forgive their sins and heal their land.
>
> 2 Chronicles 7:14

This prophecy is directed at *us,* God's people, who are called by His name. God is speaking of people with a genuine commitment to Him. He is promising us that if we turn to Him in repentance and in faith, He will hear, forgive, and heal. All His might and power and promises are for us!

Returning to God, however, is serious business. Our behavior has to indicate that we mean it. Returning to God may mean turning down a cocktail on an airplane, even when it is free and is offered for the sixth time. It means standing up for godly principles in our homes, our communities, on our jobs—even in our churches. It means really putting God first.

Sometimes all alone in my four-wheel drive I bump up the side of

Mount Princeton to the end of the road, then take a rocky ravine up as far as I can go. I leave the car and sit on one of the massive rocks in the wilderness, admiring the magnificent blue sky and smelling the freshness of the golden aspens and the pungent junipers. Off to the horizon the mountains, like ocean waves, roll on into the distance. Except for the sound of the chipmunks scurrying at my feet, everything is silent. And I imagine God, at the beginning of time, mapping everything out and then speaking it into being—having a wonderful time creating all the beauty of this earth for His children to enjoy! I feel as if I have a front seat on the dawn of Creation!

> I was there when he established the heavens and formed the great springs in the depths of the oceans. I was there when he set the limits of the seas and gave them his instructions not to spread beyond their boundaries. I was there when he made the blueprint for the earth and oceans. I was always at his side like a little child. I was his constant delight, laughing and playing in his presence. And how happy I was with what he created—his wide world and all his family of mankind! And so, young men, listen to me, for how happy are all who follow my instructions.
>
> Proverbs 8:27–32

One of the high points of my career was the Twentieth Anniversary celebration of the Home Interiors where we managed to have both Bob Hope and Billy Graham as speakers. But what pleased me most were the eleven thousand Home Interiors' Displayers who traveled from all parts of the nation to come to Dallas to celebrate—women who were God's people, who had chosen God's wisdom for their lives. They filled the Convention Center to overflowing and each face glowed with the joy of God's blessing.

And then Dr. Graham spoke. "Mothers," he said, "have the greatest job in the world, and the most fulfilling one. Always say, 'I'm a housewife and a mother and I'm proud of it,' " he exhorted them. He told how his own wife, Ruth, had had the greatest part of the responsibility of rearing their own children (five), since he'd had to travel so much over the years.

"She had the Bible in one hand and a switch in the other," he said. "And now all of them are grown and know the Lord."

Will you choose wisdom for yourself and for your family? Will you learn to be His people? Are you willing to set your goals and discipline yourself to pursue them? It is true that there are many negative forces operating in this world. But God created us to be happy and victorious. He did not intend for us to be defeated by forces that we think we cannot control. His Word tells us that He has given us power over all the forces of evil. With His divine help, we cannot fail!

This poem was written by my good friend Heartsill Wilson:

THE CHALLENGE

Blessed is the one, indeed,
Who in this life can find;
A PURPOSE that can fill his days,
And GOALS to fill his mind!

The world is filled with little people,
Content with where they are;
Not knowing joys success can bring,
No WILL to go that far!

Yet, in this world there is a need,
For some to lead the rest
To rise above the "average" life,
By giving of their best!

Would you be one, who dares to try,
When challenged by the task;
To rise to heights you've never seen,
Or is that too much to ask?

This is your day—a world to win,
Great purpose to achieve;
Accept the challenge of your goals
And in yourself, BELIEVE!

You will be proud of what you've done,
When at the close of day;
You look back on your battles, won,
Content, you came this way!

DR. HEARTSILL WILSON

11

Which Path Will Your Children Choose?

Teach a child to choose the right path, and when he is older he will remain upon it.

Proverbs 22:6

There was once a very wise father who gave his son a Bible as he was leaving to attend his first year of college.

"Jim," he said, "this book contains all the answers to your problems. It will meet all your needs." Later Jim placed the Bible on the shelf in his dorm, where it began to gather dust. Then he proceeded to major in having a good time. By the end of the six weeks he had spent his entire allowance for the whole semester. Finally he wrote to his father, asking for more money. The days passed, with no letter and no check. Jim wrote again. Still no answer. Finally in desperation, he pulled his dusty Bible off the shelf and opened it. To his amazement, out fell a twenty-dollar bill. In a moment Jim realized that his father, in his wisdom, had foreseen his need and had provided in advance for the need to be met, when Jim looked in the right place.

Even so our Heavenly Father has provided the answers to our problems and needs through His Holy Word, the Bible. Through diligent study, through knocking and seeking, the door to the wisdom contained in God's Word is opened to us. We are told in Proverbs that if we teach our children to choose the right path, when they are older they will remain upon it. Let's take a look at some of the ways in which we can encourage our children to seek God's wisdom.

Have great expectations. Always expect your child to do the right thing. Practicing faith in your children does require some risk taking on your part. You have to allow your children to do things for themselves, and that always involves the risk of failure. But even if you do everything for them you will not protect them from defeat; you will only make them totally dependent on you, and that is total failure. Don't be afraid to untie the apron strings. Remember that you must release your children to become free adults before they can ever return to you of their own accord in a voluntary relationship. Encourage your children to be independent, and expect them to win. Let them know the feeling of accomplishment that comes only through hard work and achievement. Don't ever hand them a manufactured success; you will only rob them of the thrill of accomplishment. Help them to become winners. They will feel like somebodies when they win, even though they know that you helped do some of the pushing.

Don't be permissive. Genuine love is not permissive. If God's love had been permissive, He would have given us the Ten Suggestions instead of the Ten Commandments. God is a strict Father, and He demands obedience.

> If you refuse to discipline your son, it proves you don't love him; for if you love him you will be prompt to punish him.
> Proverbs 13:24

This advice is as good now as it was in Solomon's day. If we make excuses or overprotect, we are teaching our children to escape their responsibilities. When they are grown they may continue trying to escape responsibility through drugs or alcohol. If you never teach them that the world does not owe them a living, they may never have the desire to work when they are grown.

It is important for your children to understand that the rules of your household do not depend on what rules apply in other homes. Children are little opportunists. They are quick to point out that "Tommy's mother doesn't make him do that." In a positive way you must let your children know that you have goals in mind for them which do not hinge on what other families do or don't do.

Sanctify yourself. Be the very best Christian possible. Your success or failure in life is the model for your children's behavior. If they see you putting God first, they will want to do so as well. To sanctify yourself you must pray without ceasing and keep your focus on God.

A delightful little book, written in the seventeenth century, tells of the wonders that came about in the life of an unlettered French monk, who actually did keep his heart centered on God every minute of the day through constant prayer. The *Practice of the Presence of God* tells us that when Brother Lawrence first asked permission to join the religious order, the monks told him he was too ignorant. They could accept him only to work as a cook. But Brother Lawrence accepted, happy just to work among his pots and pans. By doing menial physical work, he was able to keep his mind free so that he could pray constantly. Soon his spirit of love became so noticeable that people were traveling from all over Europe to visit the monk who "practiced the presence" so faithfully. Today it is the name of Brother Lawrence, and not those of his educated brothers, that is preserved from that monastery.

If you want your children to see Jesus in you, you must take time to pray. No matter how busy you are, God gives enough time for you to have a regular prayer time plus little short prayers during your busy day. If you take time the first thing in the morning to honor God, you will find that your time is multiplied.

Reverence for God adds hours to each day . . . .
Proverbs 10:27

We must remember that our children are constantly seeking meaning and purpose in their lives. They are seeking reality, and many look for it in the wrong places. Some fall from faith, even though we have tried very hard to rear them in it. Sometimes this happens because they don't see that faith operating very well in us. Others rebel against church ritual or pull away from family traditions as part of their natural adolescent rebellion. Many a child must "climb fool's mountain" before he finally returns to the faith of his parents.

Still, we have God's promise that when a child is taught to choose the right path, when he is older, he will remain upon it. With God-given wisdom and through the guidance of the Holy Spirit we can teach and guide and lead and mold our children in a way that will prepare them for real success. If we "practice the presence" of God as an example to our children, it is likely that they will catch our priorities and adopt them for their own.

And we must be careful to practice our priorities all the time, and not just when we think someone may be watching. For example, I feel it is important for me always to go to church, even when I am traveling and tired. Often it would be much easier to stay in the motel room and watch a worship service on television than to go to a strange church. But in the hotels where I usually stay, the people know that I claim to be Christian. And so I have a responsibility to demonstrate Christian priorities to these people, as well as to the other guests. And of course my first responsibility is to God—and to obey *His* instructions.

Being God-centered can do a great deal for the way you feel, too. One of my managers told me that she had gone through a period of such fatigue that she was unable to make decisions, until she read Francis and Edith Schaeffer's book *Everybody Can Know.* After reading it she felt like a new woman.

"For a long time I had been so depressed that it had even been hard for me to cook a meal. Besides, I thought my time was too valuable to spend all those hours in the kitchen. Selfishly, I didn't see why the family had to eat, eat, eat.

"The night I read about the resurrected Christ, I suddenly realized that if He could be concerned with my physical needs, then I must be concerned for the needs of the family that He had given to me.

"When I began to think of myself as a channel of God's love," she went on, "I found it no problem to cook any more. Now, thank the Lord, I can once again think, feel, love, and communicate."

God's Holy Spirit, His wisdom, and His love are available to us at all times to help us in the great task He has given us as mothers. With His help we can make the difference in whether our children choose to love goodness or evil, guiding them day by day into the paths of right decision and joyful living.

Yes, we do need everyday help in rearing our children, and let me introduce you to a wonderful woman, Nita Barker, who learned through great disappointment that God truly does have a plan for each life and that His plan can lead to greater victories.

Nita had suffered and shared a great disappointment and grief with a beautiful daughter whose groom-to-be was killed in an accident shortly before the planned wedding. Nita was feeling numb and restless when she was introduced to the Home Interiors family and subsequently became my protegé. Nita has a great supportive husband and three grown children—now all happily married—and seven grandchildren.

Nita is also an Area Manager with a tremendous responsibility for the training and growth of over six thousand women in Texas, Louisiana, and Tennessee. She is a very important part of our Executive Management—a wonderful example of what God can do through a woman—and through disappointment. Nita declares:

Working through Proverbs has helped me to be a better leader because I realize the importance of wisdom and understanding. To increase learning and accept instruction makes my job easier and more pleasurable.

To love the Lord gives me mercy, honor, truth, and an understanding heart when dealing with people. Through Proverbs, I am reminded to be kind, yet strong, and expect great things.

Putting the Lord first, and having Him as a partner in my business, I have the strength, the confidence, and the faith I need to make decisions, and to help people achieve their goals. I know that because God is the center of my life, I am a better wife, mother, and grandmother.

Praise the Lord!

12

A Time to Give

*Reverence for God gives a man deep strength; his children have
a place of refuge and security.*

Proverbs 14:26

Every Christmas I am dismayed again by the holiday ads that seem
to be shrieking to the world: *You must exchange gifts! Be sure you give
as much as you get!* Such a commercial approach completely obscures
the true significance of Christmas. The merchants who advertise their
products and goods for sale with such fervor seem to have missed the
whole point of this sacred holiday, on which we celebrate God's gift of
His Son to the world—a gift that asks nothing in return except that we
just receive Him. And it is only when we can grasp the fact that God
wants us to give of ourselves to others, just as He gave His Son to us,
that we can truly enjoy giving and receiving the symbolic gifts that are
a part of our Christmas tradition. The tradition is meaningless unless
we understand the purpose.

Susannah Wesley, mother of John and Charles Wesley, was a woman
who truly knew how to give of herself under all circumstances. Although she had the responsibility of rearing and caring for thirteen
children, she also furnished most of the income for her family by taking
in other people's laundry. Faced with this kind of drudgery, many of us
would just throw up our hands and let the kids rear themselves. But not
Susannah Wesley!

Susannah had a system. She set aside one hour each day to give
completely to one of her children. Every thirteen days, each child
received the priceless gift of one entire hour of his mother's time. Both
of her famous sons later said that the hour they spent alone with their

mother—a time when they were permitted to decide how the time would be spent—was special for these were the hours in which God's plan for their lives was unfolded.

Do you suppose that Susannah Wesley's house was always spotlessly clean, that the floors were always waxed, and the windows always sparkling? It is not likely. But the interesting thing is that when people are asked what they most cherished about their mothers, the reply never is "her neat, clean house." They are more likely to recall the times she spent with them when they were children, or the special things she did for them. If you want your children to have security, give them the gift of yourself, instilled with reverence for God.

It is the gift of *self* that is essential. We should not keep house just for the sake of the house. We must do our cleaning chores with our family's welfare in mind. We must be neat and clean enough to make time for our families. Our children need our presence more than they need our presents.

Everything we do as mothers must be judged by what is best for our children. When my children were in high school and I was working full time, I kept two calendars that had space for writing in appointments. I carried one in my purse and the other stayed right beside the phone at home. It was the responsibility of my two children, Don and Ruthie, to write in the school activities they wanted me to attend. These commitments were just as important to me as were the business appointments that I scheduled as a Stanley dealer and for gift shows. They had a responsibility, however, to give me plenty of advance notice. They had to realize that my time was valuable, too, and that although they were an important part of the family, they were not the only part. In this way they learned to accept some responsibility for getting me to do what they wanted, and to discharge their responsibility in a businesslike way.

One of our managers, Betty Goertzen, Fresno, California, has a son who is confined to a wheelchair. Betty's story is a unique example of what God's purpose can do in a life. She and her husband, Elvin, were used to a life-style supported by two incomes. When the opportunity presented itself to adopt a baby girl, Betty gave four-days notice to the telephone company and assumed the role of mother. They had been unable to have children naturally until this time. Seventeen months later another special child was added to their family. Listen as she tells her own story:

Our son, Bryan, was born to us with great difficulty. He suffered damage to the motor part of his brain, which is called cerebral palsy. By the time he was nine months old, it was apparent that he needed daily physical therapy. When he was one year old, I was introduced to Barbara Hammond, my manager. She was so in love with this great company that I was excited and curious about the opportunity to earn the money we needed to pay medical bills, and still be home with my children during the day. My husband was great about baby-sitting in the evenings while I held shows, and I fell in love with selling Home Interiors. Then Barbara convinced me I should attend my first seminar and meet Mary Crowley, which I did. I had only been in the business three months, so did not get to go on stage with the other winners.

My first seminar in 1965 was so exciting (seminars were smaller then), I knew I must attend again. Mary talked about how you are "somebody" and God has an exciting plan for your life. After her inspiring talks, I knew she certainly would have some advice on praying for the miracle I needed–healing for my son. At the conclusion of our second seminar in San Francisco in 1966, Elvin and I were with a group in a hospitality suite when I approached and asked Mrs. Crowley, "How do you pray for a miracle?" Bryan was to undergo surgery the following week. She smiled and graciously asked me if we minded waiting for a few moments, until the other guests had left–then she would chat with us. As a young Displayer, I had no idea of the imposition I had just placed on her. She must have been weary, but the gentle smile and sparkle in her eye gave no hint. I'll never forget her patience, her attentive listening ear, and her carefully selected words of wisdom. After a precious time together, the three of us shared in prayer for our "miracle"–not for healing necessarily–but for our acceptance. For the first time, Elvin and I completely gave Bryan to the Lord. That evening, as we departed, we were uplifted and eager to begin anew. What an added inspiration it was to us the next morning, when our hotel-room phone rang, and Mary Crowley was on the other end. The precious president of my new company cared enough to call me and share one more verse of Scripture she felt would help us meet our challenge. How very dear are my memories of that 1966 seminar!

It was the encouragement I needed because somehow I had drifted from God, but His influence by the "circle of love" from my new Home Interiors family was God's love pulling me back. That's where I started to learn how to be a winner in every area of my life. I won the beautiful punch bowl, a trip to Hawaii, and gorgeous mink as National Queen of Displayers. As I look back, only through God's goodness and the opportunity He gave us through Home Interiors was all this possible. In the meantime, Bryan required daily therapy; Kandi was only two-and-one-half years old, and I held three-to-four shows a week. We all learned how to place our priorities and to be grateful for everything. Today, Kandi is seventeen and Bryan is fifteen and a half. We have witnessed countless miracles. Bryan operates an electric wheelchair with his head, participating in wheelchair races for the orthopedic handicapped. He cannot walk or feed himself, but has been used as an example of a child with a good self-image. Kandi, who had to help me so much so we could care for Bryan, is a beautiful girl who loves the Lord and who was crowned Ideal Miss for Fresno City in 1976. My husband, Elvin, is our Rock of Gibraltar, a dependable husband and father, always willing to fill in where needed. We have learned to work together as a family.

I became a unit manager, senior manager, and finally my dream of branch manager was realized in 1976. Through all this, Mary has continued to influence our lives with her love of the Lord and today through her testimony and teaching, He is my Leader. Other people's lives are being influenced now and the miracle continues.

I admire Betty very much because she has never used her situation as an excuse for not doing her job. Betty realized that to allow her son to become the center of attention would destroy him. He is important and loved, but he also has the responsibility of sharing his mother with others.

It is important to start teaching your children when they are young that they cannot expect you to always do everything for them. By the time my children were nine and eleven they were both on allowances that would cover school lunches and supplies, activities and tithes. They had complete responsibility for managing their own money. If they got careless and spent it all before the week was over, they had to do without. In this way they learned to make choices and decisions and to accept the responsibility for them. I believe the reason that both my children are excellent money managers today is that they learned valuable lessons in managing their own money as children.

Many mothers who are busy with many responsibilities tend to over-give to their children in order to compensate for the amount of time they cannot give. This is a dangerous practice. If your children need your attention, you must make time for them and not substitute money or things. Learn to give quality time, as Susannah Wesley did, and let your children learn responsibility for themselves.

It's no fun to be a rebel's father.
Proverbs 17:21

How true. It's no fun to be a rebel's mother, either. Children who don't learn that they also have duties often become rebels or helpless adults.

Once I helped a certain young man to obtain a bank loan to buy a valuable musical instrument. One day the bank called me and told me he was three months behind in his payments. When I called him about it, he seemed surprised. Surprised that the matter had slipped his mind, and surprised that the bank was upset. It was apparent that this young man had not learned anything about financial responsibility and, consequently, had the makings of a financially irresponsible person. I quickly pointed out to him that he had a commitment to keep—to me as well as to the bank—and that if he established the practice of paying what he owed when he owed it, he would have as valuable a credit rating as a millionaire. My grandmother taught me this lesson as a young child.

I believe children should learn to have real appreciation for the special things that are done for them and that they should be expected to show that appreciation. But even more than that, they need to learn that they have a responsibility to the people who help them. They need to learn to speak their thanks and to show their gratitude by their behavior.

We parents, however, need to be sure that we do not find ourselves in the position where we need the praise and thanks of others and get our feelings hurt when it doesn't come. When we see ourselves made in the image and likeness of God, we are able to have a good self-image and an abundance of self-esteem that makes us able to enjoy receiving the approval of others, without finding it a necessity, because we find God's love is sufficient to meet all our needs.

It is essential to see that communication is kept open between your children and you, and this responsibility is yours. You must do a lot of listening, if you want to understand what teenagers are trying to say. Sometimes they will ask a dozen questions that have nothing to do with what they are really thinking. If you turn them off, you may never get another chance to hear about a problem, or a decision with which they are wrestling.

If a child asks an irrelevant question, you might say, "That's a very good question. What else did you have in mind about it?" Be sure that you are positive and encouraging, rather than suspicious and critical. Your attitude can make the difference in whether your child is able to communicate with you or not.

Another way to open communication is to make cheerfulness a habit, even when you don't feel enthusiastic. If you exhibit cheerfulness that you don't feel, you are not being insincere. You are merely making a conscious effort to change one little area of your behavior in order to reach your goal of better communication. You may be pretending cheerfulness that you do not feel, but if you keep on pretending, your self-image will improve. Soon it will be a more natural thing to be cheerful.

> When a man is gloomy, everything seems to go wrong; when
> he is cheerful, everything seems right!
>
> Proverbs 15:15

Sometimes we improve communication with our children when we admit that we are really not an authority on everything. Don't be afraid to simply say, "I really don't know what is best for you to do." God does know the answer, so encourage your child to commit his work to the Lord and ask God for wisdom. God honors *preparation, prayer,* and *persistence*. In making decisions, remember that the Lord grants wisdom, and He does it through the marvelous minds He has given us.

A helpful way to reach a decision is to write down all the alternatives, and then prayerfully consider the various details of the situation and the possible consequences of each decision we might make. It is true that God already knows what our thoughts are, but it will help us to clarify them in our own minds, if we write them down. Then we can ask God to give us a better idea. Sometimes the answer won't come right away, and we will have to wait for additional facts or for God's timing. At other times, God's will is for us to just be quiet and listen to others. Many times we learn more when we listen than when we talk.

> A wise man holds his tongue. Only a fool blurts out everything
> he knows; that only leads to sorrow and trouble.
>
> Proverbs 10:14

God does have the answers. When we look to Him for wisdom and guidance in decision making, we often find that the answer is revealed to us in a moment of time, maybe in the middle of the night, when we are suddenly awakened out of a sound sleep. It is essential for our children's sake that they see us trusting God in making decisions and not leaning unto our own understanding.

When my children were small, bedtime was a precious time of day because it was when we would have our daily prayer time together. It was especially meaningful to me on the days when I had to discipline them and they were unhappy. Kneeling together by the side of the bed, when the air was laden with tension, was more beneficial than the best medicine ever discovered.

Yes, prayer heals. It smoothes out family differences. But prayer cannot work, if it is only an empty ritual. You can't just scream at one another all day long and then—suddenly—decide to pray. Prayer must be a part of the fabric of family life. We have to develop a strong bond by communicating with God regularly as a family—on all the good days as well as on the less-perfect ones. We must let our families know that we depend on God. We must be able to say with Joshua, "As for me and my house, we will serve the Lord."

Lydia is one of my Bible models. She was a professional saleswoman, a businesswoman, a merchant who sold quality purple goods. In Acts 16 we read the story of how Paul met Lydia and the other women with whom she was worshiping on the banks of the river in Philippi. These women had not heard of the Messiah, but their hearts were open. They were worshiping God as best they knew. When Paul told them that the Messiah had come and had died for them that they might have life, Lydia believed. She was baptized that very moment with all her household, and became the first convert on the continent of Europe. Paul later wrote his great letter of rejoicing to the Philippians who had helped him in his missionary work. This letter is a part of the Bible today because Lydia was open to God. She was a learner and a leader.

God does give something special to the lives of our children when we really give them to Him, and then discharge our commitment to bring them up in the nurture and admonition of the Lord, faithfully teaching them from the Word of God and trusting Him to guide their lives.

We must be rich toward God, even as He has been rich toward us. We must remain close to Him and have a real desire to worship Him—a real hunger for His Word. We must trust Him with our children, even as He has trusted us with them. Then—and only then—will the gift of ourselves given to our children be a truly blessed one, bearing much fruit. And as Proverbs 31 declares ". . . [they] will rise up and call us blessed" (*see* v. 28 KJV).

13

The Joy of Work

Commit your work to the Lord, then it will succeed.
Proverbs 16:3

> Now I lay me down to sleep—
> I pray Thee, Lord, my soul to keep.
> If I should die before I wake,
> I pray Thee, Lord, my soul to take.

Most of us learned this familiar childhood prayer at a very young age. Few, however, are familiar with the second verse.

> Now I wake me up to work—
> I pray Thee, Lord, I do not shirk.
> If I should die before tonight,
> I pray Thee, Lord, my work's all right.

Our forefathers knew the necessity of working hard as well as the value of a job well done. They never worried about how to spend their leisure time, because they never had any!

When training new managers at my Colorado mountain home, I often let my eyes come to rest on the tree-covered slope beyond the wooden deck outside my living room. Sometimes I will see a chipmunk storing pine nuts in the cupboards of his cheeks. He stuffs in so many that soon his little cheeks are pouched out like soft-sided luggage on a trip to Europe! He can hardly scamper about without falling over, as he hurries to store up food for winter. Nature itself has endowed the tiny chipmunk with the urge for self-preservation and the compulsion to provide for himself by working to gather food for the cold months ahead.

People sometimes say that because the world is in such bad shape, it's a sure sign that Jesus is going to come again soon, so they'll just sit down and wait for Him. How foolish! Jesus will come according to *His* timetable, and I, for one, prefer to be busy working. Remember what the shepherds were doing when the great light shone out to announce Jesus' birth? They were tending their flocks by night, doing their jobs. And what was Moses doing when God came to him and told him He was going to make him a great leader? He was guarding the sheep. None of those to whom God appeared was sitting around idle and useless. They were all working.

God intends for us to work. Our labors should be rewarding, whether we are compensated for them or not. We must find joy in the work we do, whether we work at home or in a career. Then our work will not be a burden to us, and we will be free to really enjoy whatever other compensation it affords.

Unfortunately, many women today have the impression that the only kind of work that counts is a career. To be successful, we are urged to become aggressive. We are encouraged to adopt all the bad traits of men and none of the good ones.

We women need to realize that for us success is a moving target. Our goals toward working outside the home frequently change, depending on our circumstances. When children are young, we may want to work outside the home just enough to earn some extra money for an occasional baby-sitter, or a professional hairdo, or we may need to work for economic reasons. Later, as children grow up, we may want to work enough to help pay for their educations. Finally, when they are out of the nest, we often feel that we need a career for our own personal fulfillment.

There was a time when I chose not to recruit mothers of preschool children for Home Interiors. But then, after going into many different homes, I realized that the quantity of time a mother spends with her family is not nearly as important as the *quality* of time spent in bringing up happy, well-adjusted children. Many young women become better mothers by being able to escape the terrible *D's*—*debts, diapers,* and *dishes*—for a few hours every week. It is far better for a young mother to work part-time than to stay at home bored, spending thirty hours a week in the fantasy world of television soap operas, as many do. Nagging, self-pity, resentment—even child abuse, pill-popping and alcoholism—are sometimes the tragic results of an unhappy young mother's feeling unfulfilled and trapped at home. We do recognize, however, the importance of a mother (or father) being home when a child comes home from school. One of the advantages of our type of work for women is the ability to set their own working hours, so they *can* be home when children come home from school to share that precious time with a growing, unfolding mind and emotion of childhood.

Work is especially valuable to the woman whose children are grown. With her nest empty she actually needs to work—otherwise she is likely to become self-centered. She'll feel hurt because her kids don't come to see her as often as she feels they should. She will develop ills, aches, and pains, becoming so touchy that it will be almost impossible not to upset her.

Today many women have their last child in school by their early thirties and out of school in their midforties. Since the life expectancy for young women today is estimated to be over seventy years, most mothers will have about a quarter of a century, after their children are gone, in which it will be rewarding for them to work outside the home.

One of my managers, who was in her thirties, was complaining to me that she would never be able to have a real career because she had started too late. She felt that she had to waste ten years of her life in part-time work while she took care of her three small children. And now it was too late to start a career.

I had to smile, as I pointed out to her that I had started Home Interiors when I was forty-two. I added that since that time, the company has grown into a multimillion dollar corporation and I have had a wonderful career!

Commit your work to the Lord, then it will succeed.

Proverbs 16:3

When I founded Home Interiors, I made sure the company would be based on the idea of what it could give to others—to the women who sold the products, as well as to the homes where those accessories went. As I went along, I used some of the profits to help others as well, in gratitude to God who had made our success possible. I dedicated the company to the purpose of *helping others help themselves,* enabling them to find joy as well as profit in their work. The result has been that even in the rough years, I've been rich in many ways. As my dear pastor, Dr. W. A. Criswell, expressed it in our Twentieth Anniversary Book:

> If the Lord God is as good to Mary Crowley and her Home Interiors the next twenty years, as He has been through the last twenty, we shall all be persuaded that the glorious millenium has come. Oh, the marvelous remembrances of God upon the building of this great company of dedicated people and their ministries of homes beautiful!

Then, after the Twentieth Anniversary celebration was over, I began to receive bundles of mail from hotels, cab drivers, and many others who had come in contact with the eleven thousand women who'd attended. And they were all in agreement that ours was the greatest group of women they'd ever served.

Letters like these don't just happen. Home Interiors people are trained to be more sensitive to the needs of others because we have fostered an atmosphere of caring within the company. Our women are not demanding. They are well aware that we serve—that it is our purpose to serve, and to find joy in serving. The friendship of the people we serve is the foundation of our progress.

One letter I treasure is one I received from a nurse in Maine. It told me of what one Home Interiors' Displayer had done for someone else, when she'd committed her work to the Lord. The Displayer, Linda Navelski, had gone to a hospital to receive treatment as an outpatient, and while there, she met an eighty-one-year-old woman named Lorena. The Displayer soon learned that Lorena had been in the hospital for two months with a terminal illness, and during the entire time, had not received a single visitor. The poor old lady had no relatives at all. The Displayer came back, bringing Lorena a gift—a brass candleholder with a beautiful candle. It was then that the nurse saw Lorena smile for the first time in months. "The decorator lady is preparing me to be heaven's decorator," Lorena told the nurse with a new spark in her eyes.

After that, the "decorator lady" visited Lorena every week, always bringing a gift of more candles. The nurse noticed that Lorena and the decorator lady always talked a long time, and afterward Lorena would seem much happier.

At last, when Lorena was near death, she asked the nurse to call the decorator lady, but the nurse had lost the Displayer's phone number.

"Just tell the decorator lady that when I'm in heaven, I'll decorate one corner just for her," Lorena said.

Later the nurse found a Home Interiors' folder on which was written the short note: TO LORENA. GOD LOVES YOU. The nurse looked up Home Interiors' Dallas address and wrote to thank us for what our Displayer had done to make Lorena's last days more joyful.

How beautifully the decorator lady's experience illustrates the spirit we have tried to build into Home Interiors. When I called the Displayer, I found that she was a very busy person with three small children to care for. Yet she had taken valuable time to be kind to a person she did not know, a person who could never be a customer, or benefit her in any way. Lorena was just someone who needed her, and so she served.

What a joy to use our careers as a means of helping others! God rewards us in many ways when we do His work here on earth, but the greatest reward is the knowledge that we are serving Him.

In my work I have seen many women succeed. I've also seen a few others drop out and feel like failures. Over the years I have had the opportunity to observe a few rules which, when followed, generally make people successful in their careers.

Have purpose in your work that is worthy of your best efforts. Set goals that are worthwhile, definite, and realistic (*see* chapters 6, 7). You will find that the "strength" of the purpose will take over and keep you going long after your own physical strength is depleted.

Add royalty to the routine. Find excitement in everyday work by adding a touch of royalty to it. Our slogan THINK MINK means think the best—don't think rabbit or squirrel. "Don't get the rabbit habit." Add a touch of mink to what you do—like flowers on the table—candles to make a so-so meal festive—a single flower placed on the tray taken to a member of family who is ill—a paper napkin with a butterfly on it to add color to a child's place—a thank-you gift to a hostess as you leave her home (maybe a candle in a crystal holder). Little things make a person feel like "royalty"—a note saying *"You're special"*—"I love you" in a child's lunch box or a husband's sandwich bag.

Make every day special for someone. Most everything in life tends to tarnish and we need to "polish" a lot of relationships every day.

Learn to manage time, energy, money.

Time—Oh, how terribly important is *time* management. I've found that I do better when I get the difficult jobs done *first*, then I can live the day with anticipation; otherwise, I'm living it in dread, "Oh, I dread to get started on ironing" (or whatever the different job). Live life on tiptoe—expecting great things to happen.

"Reverence for God adds hours to each day . . ." (Proverbs 10:27). So it is extremely important for me to start the day with Him.

Energy—Energy grows on energy, and apathy grows on apathy. Fifteen minutes of exercise early in the day gets my circulation going and gives me more energy to work with. Learn to delegate jobs that members of the family can do so you won't wind up "too tired" to be a loving wife. The greatest enemy of man is ego. The greatest enemy of woman is fatigue.

Money—My grandmother used to say that "a wasteful woman could throw out the back door more than a hardworking husband could bring in through the front door." It *is* especially difficult to manage money in these days of inflation, but I've learned through the years of experience with thousands of women and families that it is *attitude* that is the key to managing money and setting priorities. The most uncomfortable place to live is just beyond your income! (You can read the story of one young family's learning to live and manage money better by tithing in *Think Mink!*)

In addition to putting God first by tithing, our family also had two very important policies:

1. Nothing was ever bought on credit that would not still be valuable and usable when it was paid for. Naturally, this meant no groceries or vacation trips, and so forth, were bought on credit. Many is the time we ate very simple foods (like oatmeal) for days at a time.
2. What was bought on credit must be budgeted—allowed for and paid on as promised.

Again, to quote my grandmother, "If you pay who you owe, what you owe, when you owe it, you will have as good a credit rating as a millionaire, for that's all he can do." (Oh, yes, we got behind a time or two due to unexpected emergencies—but we always got right back to paying up—even when it meant a lot of doing without.) A sure way to *not* wind up in financial disaster is to give one-tenth to God, put one-tenth in savings, and use the rest wisely and with confidence.

Be dependable. We save both time and energy when we make a commitment to tithe. We are spared the fretting over how much to give, for we have already made that decision. The world of business is looking for people that can be depended on. Do what you are *expected* to do. Yes—when and how you are expected to do it, *plus* an attitude of wanting to do even more than the "expected."

Don't be afraid to fail. We all "fail" sometimes. Develop a sense of adventure. Naturally some of the things you attempt in life and work will not work out. Jackie Finchum, who was struck by polio at the age of two, walks only on crutches. Still, he announced that he was going to walk twenty miles for the March of Dimes, because he felt that everyone needed to show a willingness to do something for others. What if he had failed? Twenty miles is a long way even for those who walk without crutches, but Jackie achieved his goal. He was not afraid to take a chance and the Lord helped him all the way, one step at a time.

And most of us know about Babe Ruth. When he would strike out at bat, he would always tip his hat to the pitcher. "I want him to know that it's his time to worry," the Babe said. "If I keep on swinging, I'm going to connect." Even if you strike out, remember that you're not out of the game. You always have another chance. Look on your work as an adventure and you will win much of the time.

Did you ever see a football player fail to catch a pass and come off the field limping? His "loser's limp" is his excuse for not catching the ball. We must be careful that we don't adopt a loser's limp to justify our mistakes, but rather learn from them and go on.

Even when our work is committed to the Lord, we will still make mistakes. Mistakes often happen for the purpose of showing us a better way to do something. Even though we give out, we must be sure we never give up.

Be honest—with others—with your family—with yourself. Don't accept your own excuses.

We can always "prove" that we are right, but is the Lord convinced?

Proverbs 16:2

The Lord hates cheating and delights in honesty.

Proverbs 11:1

Fall in love with your work. Those who are in a career that they don't enjoy may possibly need a different job—one which offers opportunities for fulfillment rather than just a paycheck. It is much easier to commit to the Lord a job that we can become enthusiastic about. And when we truly commit our work to the Lord, we will soon know the real joy of our labors. We need spiritual energy to become leaders. Resentment, hate, unforgiveness are all nonconductors of spiritual energy—yet they affect us all at some time. Satan camps at our weak places and seeks to rob us of joy.

It is rare when a company has an heir, but Home Interiors has a real offspring in Creative Visions Corporation—not a subsidiary, nor related in any way to Home Interiors—but nonetheless, a child of our philosophy, care, and love. Let the testimony of Lynda Gail Cleveland, president of Creative Visions Corporation, tell you what the principles of Proverbs mean to her:

> *My association with Mary Crowley and Home Interiors began like so many others–rendering services to meet a need. At that time I was a high-school speech teacher and a free-lance multimedia consultant. As a media specialist, I had the opportunity to prepare the Bicentennial multimedia presentation performed for the Home Interiors seminars in 1976. During the seminars, I was to experience the fine tapestry of women who win, woven from the threads of service spun by Mary Crowley and her associates at Home Interiors. The contagious enthusiasm of these women captured my attention, and my interest in business began to flourish. Within short months, the instruction, encouragement, and gentle nudging of Mary Crowley produced results I had not dared think about earlier. At the conclusion of the 1977 school year, I traded my world of students and textbooks for the world of business and "bottom lines." I became president of my own communications production and consulting corporation.*
>
> *Mary Crowley became my on-the-job instructor, my advisor, my cheerleader, my prayer partner, my disciplinarian, my example, and–best of all–my special friend.*
>
> *After being in business one year, we have overcome obstacles, accepted challenges, and made a small profit. As I reflect upon this*

year, I am reminded that Mrs. C advised me to commit our work to the Lord and to practice four **Ps:** **Proverbs,** **Preparation,** **Prayer,** **Persistence.** *Actually, it never occurred to me that our business could do other than succeed—not because of self-confidence, but because of the faith and foundation upon which it is built. On the first evening after I knew Creative Visions would be a reality, Mrs. C and I sat together discussing the basics of business and free enterprise. She shared with me Lincoln's Ten Cannot-ments which appeared some years ago in Robert G. Lee's Sourcebook of 500 Illustrations:*

> *You cannot bring about prosperity by discontinuing thrift.*
> *You cannot help the small man by tearing down the big man.*
> *You cannot strengthen the weak by weakening the strong.*
> *You cannot lift the wage earner by pulling down the wage payer.*
> *You cannot help the poor man by destroying the rich.*
> *You cannot keep out of trouble by spending more than your income.*
> *You cannot further the brotherhood of man by inciting class hatred.*
> *You cannot establish security on borrowed money.*
> *You cannot build character and courage by taking away man's initiative and independence.*
> *You cannot help people permanently by doing for them what they could and should be doing for themselves.*

Many times since then I have felt the security and nourishment of having my business shaped by her wisdom and sealed by the bond of the prayer that we shared on that first "business meeting" of my company.

Each of us at Creative Visions has found a special joy in Monday morning devotional times together. As a company goal, we seek individually to draw daily instruction on living and business principles from the chapter corresponding to the day of the month found in our policy book, Proverbs.

During the past year, through Mary and Dave Crowley, Don Carter, and each of the Area Managers I have learned a new meaning of winning. In times rich with laughter and fun, in the warmth of a special moment shared, and in the consoling tears at the loss of my dad, I have been sustained by the love and prayers of many friends

Home Interiors, who not only believe the promise of Proverbs 3:6, but who embody its practice.

Creative Visions had the opportunity to design and coordinate the Twentieth Anniversary Souvenir Book, the Program, and Songbook. The interchange between the two staffs of Home Interiors and Creative Visions was a testimony to the spirit of teamwork each experienced as we sought a common goal. While engaged in our project, I discovered these lines which have taken on rich significance and serve as an influence to my daily walk.

> *Think deeply,*
> *Speak gently,*
> *Love much,*
> *Laugh often,*
> *Work hard,*
> *Give freely,*
> *Pay promptly,*
> *Pray earnestly,*
> *And be kind.*

Few young leaders have the opportunity of being heir to the riches in experience of not only one successful career, but also of the gains realized by the support of an entire company, such as I have enjoyed with Home Interiors.

As I studied the Home Interiors tapestry in 1976, I marveled at the beauty that is possible when the principles of Christian living and business are woven together. How exciting it is to know that the same fiber in the hands of the same Designer can render an equally beautiful finished piece with its own unique image for Creative Visions.

. . . This one thing I know—God is for me!

Psalms 56:9

14

Not If Only—But Next Time

He who loves wisdom loves his own best interest and will be a success.

Proverbs 19:8

When the Home Interiors' National Queen of Displayers stepped up to the microphone during our Twentieth Anniversary celebration, she said, repeating a familiar quotation, "Through working for Home Interiors, I've learned this: what we are is God's gift to us; what we become is our gift to God."

With that philosophy this lady had become a super saleswoman. Among the thousands of successful women in the organization she had reached the top. In the process, she had developed a winning personality and an ability to serve.

"In Home Interiors I learned to set goals and to follow the basic company guidelines," she said. "Then I worked the best I could all week, every week."

She had followed the very same plans that were available to everyone else. No secret formulas were hers. She'd recognized that God had given her a potential and she'd trusted Him to develop and refine that gift, as she worked diligently and faithfully.

So many people are always looking back and saying, "*If only* I'd done this [or that], I could have been successful." And it is this very attitude which may be destroying their chances for success. Winners never look to the past, except to learn from it. Rather, they make goals for the future and say, "*Next time* I will do better."

When one particular Home Interiors Displayer made up her mind that she really wanted to be queen, she set her goal and then visualized it in a very concrete way. She hung a picture of the previous year's winner on her wall, then pasted her own picture over the queen's face. All year she kept looking at the crown which rested on her own head in the queen's picture and kept on working as hard as she could. And the next year—you guessed it—she became queen!

Some people would say it's not humble to want to be queen. There are those who say it's immodest to want to excel and be outstanding. But that's not what the Bible says.

> He who loves wisdom loves his own best interests and will be
> a success.
>
> Proverbs 19:8

God wants us to succeed. He tells us that we should love our own best interests. He also tells us that it is in our own best interest to learn to love and serve others. Add to this a good sense of humor, a big dose of patience—and a dash of humility—and you will be rewarded manyfold.

Many women who seek shortcuts to success find the way intersected by beguiling streets, which turn out to be dead ends or crossroads. They appear to be smoother than the direct route but quickly turn washboard-rough, and these women wind up full of self-pity—a deadly disease. The main highway to success may not be too clearly marked, so let's look at some of the ways which we have learned that work for us.

I'd like you to hear from Karen Baker of Albuquerque, New Mexico, a young mother of two and wife of a school administrator. Her story illustrates what God can do through a woman who learns His plan for her success.

I was an elementary-school teacher for six years previous to my association with Home Interiors. In 1969 I resigned my position to remain home with a small son. Shortly after this, I was introduced to Home Interiors through a show in the neighborhood. I needed to supplement our income, so I inquired into the possibilities of becoming a Displayer. What impressed me most was the fact that she earned more money in one evening's work than I would make all day as a substitute teacher.

I had a very slow start as a business woman, until I attended a seminar at Denver in January, 1970. This was the turning point in my life and career. It was at this time that I met Mary Crowley, whose

*wise teachings and Christian philosophy influenced me beyond com-
pare. Here was a woman who stood up and talked about God's love
with sincerity. She seemed to run her company the same way. Being
impressed and inspired, I wanted to become more involved with this
successful company, based on these principles. My promotion to unit
manager came in July 1970. Then came senior management, and finally my promotion to branch manager in January 1977.*

*My family, consisting of my wonderful husband of sixteen years,
Ronnie; a son, Gary, age ten; and daughter, Melissa, age eight, have
given me their love, encouragement, and support throughout my
career. I feel very blessed to be able to be a wife, mother, and to have
such an interesting, fulfilling career.*

*A minister once said that in the Psalms the Lord is teaching us how
to get along with Him; and in the Proverbs, the Lord is teaching us how
to get along in the world. The Proverbs have become one of my favorite
books in the Bible, mainly as a result of management-training sessions,
based on the Proverbs, given by our president, Mary Crowley. Mary
has a special way of making the Scriptures come alive.*

*The Proverbs were written by King Solomon to teach his sons and
people how to live. He wanted them to be understanding, just, and fair
in everything they did. He wanted his people to be wise, and he knew
that the basis for all wisdom comes from knowing God. He knew that if
you know God, you'll know yourself. Mary knows this, too. She says,
"You've got to have your anchor in the right point." As far as I'm
concerned, getting that "anchor in," makes anyone a winner. Mary
and her Bible studies have been the main influence in my life in helping
me get my anchor in.*

*I have been fortunate enough to be associated with a company with
a purpose. A part of that purpose is focused on helping others find God
and themselves. I have learned that our God is first of all a God of love.
He wants us to have an abundant life. He wants us all to be winners.
Because He is a loving Father, He is also a disciplining Father. He
knows what is best for us. He wants us to win by His rules. Winning is
sometimes three steps forward and two steps backward, but every
cloud can have a silver lining, when you turn it over to Him. I can be
more positive because I know that God is with me now, and He has
been there before me. Because of Him, I am special—I am somebody!*

But, God and Mary had more in mind for my life. Through my association with Home Interiors, has come the privilege and respon-sibility of my being in a leadership position. I have learned that we are leaders by the nature of our performance. The Proverbs have helped me to be a leader with its teachings on how to live as a leader. With this has come another blessing: the happiness that comes in forgetting yourself by helping others. Mary has helped me learn that true happiness comes when you are helping others to achieve and become winners themselves. To do this, I must keep my priorities straight. This is not always easy. I've found that I can't do it alone. I need Him. I can really foul it up by myself; but when I let Him do it, it comes out right. He is patient and allows me to make mistakes, but His love is a stubborn love.

People marvel at the many prizes I have won with Home Interiors, but I know that my real winning has been my new relationship with God and other people.

15

Giving God the Glory

The Lord's blessing is our greatest wealth. All our work adds nothing to it!

Proverbs 10:22

How many times I was reminded during the Home Interiors' Twentieth Anniversary celebration to give God all the glory for everything: for the fantastic success of our great organization and for this momentous occasion in the history of Home Interiors. What a thrilling experience it has been to see what He is able to do with one small idea, one humble endeavor that is committed to Him!

The first chapter of Psalms tells what God promises to do for a person whose life reflects reverence and obedience, whose delight is in the law of the Lord. God likens such people to trees, deeply rooted and fruitful. He says that their leaves shall not wither, and all they do shall prosper.

Bob Hope, beloved by millions and the most famous comedian in the world, stood on a platform in the middle of the Dallas Convention Center to an eleven-thousand flashbulb salute and with typical understatement quipped, "I don't believe this. I've never seen so many gorgeous gals in my life. I wish I were six months younger!"

This great man who had entertained so many of our servicemen through the grim days of combat was being funny as usual, but there was much truth in his words. Our women *are* beautiful. They have the special, radiant beauty that comes only from trusting and serving the Lord and delighting in Him. It is a source of great joy to me to know that many of them had learned to do so through their association with Home Interiors and Gifts.

I don't believe it either, I thought as my heart surged with gratitude to my Heavenly Father who had made all this possible. As my mind traveled back twenty years through the portals of time, I was filled with a strange mixture of pride and humility, as I recalled the words to a song written by Dottie Rambo, beloved artist of gospel music and popular television performer.

> Roll back the curtain of memory now and then,
> Show me where you brought me from
> And what I might have been.
> Remember I'm human, Lord, and tend to forget,
> So remind me, remind me, dear Lord.

"In Dallas," Bob went on with his characteristic deadpan expression, "when you dial a prayer, the phone is answered by Mary Crowley."

Everyone roared. But there was no doubt in anyone's mind that Mary Crowley believed in prayer! It is no secret that Home Interiors was founded on prayer and continues to grow because of it. But God Himself was the One who had produced the radiant glow on the faces of all those wonderful women who made up the audience. He alone was responsible for their success—for our success as a company. Individually and collectively, we gave Him all the glory and praise.

How thankful I was right at that moment that I had learned to trust the Lord and to lean on Him from the beginning, to obey Him by giving Him the first 10 percent of my income regardless of how much or how little there was of it. Even at the times when it had meant having only cereal instead of meat for supper, I had wanted Him to have the firstfruits of my labors, because I knew that everything I received was His gift to me and not something I had earned.

In the third chapter of Malachi, verse 10, there is a blessing *promised* to those who honor God with their tithes. God says that we should *prove* Him by giving Him the firstfruits of our labors and that if we do this, He will open up the windows of heaven and pour out a blessing so great that we will not be able to receive it all! He invites us to put Him to the test! Surely He had been faithful in keeping this promise to me beyond anything I ever could have imagined.

We must be very careful, however, that we are tithing only out of loving obedience and *not* with any intention of bribing the Lord. Many people tithe and are rewarded with even more precious gifts than material wealth. Sometimes it is not good for us to have money, and the Lord knows what is best. Some people have been totally ruined by financial success. Many people cannot handle riches. The Lord knows who they are and, in His wisdom, does not bless them in that way. *For what shall it profit a man*, Jesus reminds us, *if he gain the whole world and lose his own soul?*

We do have God's assurance, however, that when we trust and obey Him—especially in the area of tithing—our lives will be rich with His blessings.

> Honor the Lord by giving him the first part of all your income, and he will fill your barns with wheat and barley and overflow your wine vats with the finest wines.
>
> Proverbs 3:9, 10

> Don't be conceited, sure of your own wisdom. Instead, trust and reverence the Lord, and turn your back on evil; when you do that, then you will be given renewed health and vitality.
>
> Proverbs 3:7, 8

Not long ago I had a good conversation with Victor Graham, a young friend, who is a student at the Dallas Theological Seminary. Victor and I discussed God's laws concerning giving.

"You can't outgive God," I told him. "The more you give for His purposes, the more He gives right back to you."

Victor agreed. Smiling, he told me of a great philanthropist who once said the same thing. This man was asked how come he could give away so much and have so much left. "As I shovel it out, God shovels it in. And His shovel is bigger than mine."

What a beautiful way to express God's generosity! It is expressed in another way in the Book of Proverbs:

> It is possible to give away and become richer! It is also possible to hold on too tightly and lose everything. Yes, the liberal man shall be rich! By watering others, he waters himself.
>
> Proverbs 11:24

Later I received a lovely gift from Victor, which always reminds me of our conversation. His brother-in-law, a silversmith, had made me two miniature silver shovels, one of them larger than the other. I frequently wear them on a chain around my neck as a reminder of God's faithfulness, and as a way of illustrating the point when I have an opportunity to tell others about God's laws of giving.

How sad that so many people miss out on God's blessings by not being generous. Some spend all their energy trying to figure out a way to keep the government from collecting lawful taxes, never considering their rightful responsibility. Many spend every penny on themselves, without ever thinking of the people and worthy causes their contributions could aid, or the selfish example they are setting for their children. Others are too afraid to take a step in faith and give away the first 10 percent of their income. They just don't see how they can live on what is left. People on limited incomes are often afraid that they cannot afford to tithe. Little do they realize that if they are poor, then they certainly cannot afford not to tithe. God's ways are not our ways and His arithmetic is not our arithmetic!

Anyone can afford to tithe. God somehow does more with nine-tenths of our income, after He has received the first tenth, than we could ever do with the whole amount. I do not understand how this is possible, but I know it works. "The obedience is mine, the miracle is His." God has all the resources. He wants us to have everything we need, and He is well able to supply it for "the earth is the Lord's, and the fulness thereof." Our Father is rich indeed and He said He would supply all our needs according to His riches in glory. In Luke 12:31 we are told: "He will always give you all you need from day to day if you will make the Kingdom of God your primary concern."

When World Wide Pictures first planned to make *The Hiding Place,* the movie about Corrie ten Boom's life in a concentration camp during World War II, it appeared that there would just not be enough money to produce the film. Bill Brown, president of World Wide Pictures, was meeting with Corrie ten Boom along with Cliff Barrows, Billy and Ruth Graham, and others, planning the film, if they could get the money together. Everyone was feeling very discouraged. Everyone, that is, except Corrie. This beautiful lady, who had had so much experience in trusting God under the most painful and frightening circumstances for her daily needs and for her very survival, and who had seen her simple, childlike faith rewarded by one miracle after another, was not worried. "Don't worry," she reassured them. "My Father owns all the cattle on a thousand hills."

The planning meeting wasn't sure how or when but they somehow got the impression that Corrie's Father was more real to her than anyone else and that He knew exactly what was going on. That evening they prayed that if God wanted the movie made, the money would come. The very next day Corrie arrived wearing a big smile and showed a check for fifty thousand dollars which had just come in the mail from a *Texas cattleman*.

"See, I told you," Corrie crowed. "My Heavenly Father just sold a few cows!"

When we give our finances to Jesus, He does something with them that we cannot fathom. He even makes our mistakes turn out right. I am reminded of something that happened several years ago, when a friend told me about a "worthy cause" that turned out to be a rather expensive proposition for me. Someone was in real need, and I kept getting more and more involved, and finally lost quite a lot of money. I was truly irritated at myself, because I am aware that all my money is really God's money and He expects me to be a good steward. But let me tell you what the Lord did with my mistake!

At about the same time, a small Dallas movie company wanted to make a good, clean family film and they needed investors. I decided to get involved—not because I wanted a return on my investment—but because I knew these sincere young men wanted to make a decent movie at a time when families could hardly find a single family picture to take their children to see. And so I invested in their project.

Three years later I began to receive royalty checks. The amounts were staggering. I'd more than made up the money I had lost in trying to befriend a good person (but who had badly mismanaged her business). I was making a profit that I really did not need or expect—and all because of a sweet little terrier named *Benji,* who starred in a movie which quickly became a worldwide hit! Benji's success lent further emphasis to the wonderful truth that I already had learned: You just cannot outgive God!

> Bring all the tithes into the storehouse so that there will be food enough in my Temple; if you do, I will open up the windows of heaven for you and pour out a blessing so great that you won't have room enough to take it in! Try it! Let me prove it to you!
>
> Malachi 3:10

A giving, sharing attitude comes from the heart. When we have it, we are more aware of the other person's need than we are of what we may have to sacrifice. God is able to give us this attitude, when we commit to Him all that we are and all that we have. The first miracle of generosity takes place in the heart.

There is a story of a man in India who traveled three hundred dusty miles over dirt roads to visit a friend, bringing with him an inexpensive gift.

"Do you mean to say you made that long and tiring journey just to bring me this gift?" the friend asked in amazement.

"Yes," the young man replied. "The long, weary journey was a part of the gift."

In their excellent book *What Every Woman Still Knows,* Millie Cooper and Martha Fanning tell this story in different settings but the emphasis is the same.

That's the difference between giving and sharing. We must be sure we do not wait until we have an abundance from which to give and *then* make donations of the leftovers. An essential ingredient in sharing is *sacrifice.* This truth is evident in the story of the widow's mite. Jesus said that because the poor widow had given all that she had out of her need, she had given far more than the others who had given out of their abundance. The meaning of sharing is again beautifully expressed in the words of Christ from *The Vision of Sir Launfal:*

> Not what we give, but what we share—
> For the gift without the giver is bare;
> Who gives himself with his alms feeds three—
> Himself, his hungering neighbor and Me.
> JAMES RUSSELL LOWELL

Something exciting begins to happen when people start tithing in obedience to God. Eventually, many are able to give away as much as 20 or 30 percent, as God makes this generosity possible, and wonderful things begin to happen in their lives. They find that God is true to His word, and that there is real blessing in doing things His way. My family and I have found God's plan is the best.

Of course, we do have to remember to be good stewards of what God has given us. We have to pray to discover the best use of His money, and that means we cannot give to everyone who asks. Many requests come from organizations where very little of the contributions received goes to pay for anything other than salaries and overhead expenses of professional fund raisers.

I prefer to contribute to organizations that I know about personally. I always try to learn the facts about the charities to which I am considering making a donation. I don't feel the least bit guilty about asking questions concerning how the money will be spent. After I have done my homework, I pray and ask the Lord which ones He feels are worthy and effective.

If we truly wish to start being generous to others, we must first overcome the old habits of thinking of ourselves first. Many people make a commitment to live a Christian life and then right away allow Satan to rob them of the joys they should be reaping. The "enemy" doesn't have to cause some startling circumstance to convince us to break our promises. Usually all he has to do is put us under condemnation by causing us to become discouraged. If he can make us doubt our commitment, or get us involved in a guilt trip because of some failure on our part, he is often able to sidetrack us from God's purpose for our lives.

How much better just to trust the Lord, as Ethel Waters did. Although she came from obscurity into great fame and fortune, this great lady never wavered in her faith in God. At her funeral I watched the sorrowing masses who mourned her, and once again marveled at what God is able to do for those who are committed to Him.

This famous singer was born in a slum section outside Philadelphia to a young, black girl of thirteen who was unwed and the victim of rape. In the eyes of the world, never was any child more unwanted. But in *God's* eyes, no child is unwanted, ever.

Ethel Waters spent a lifetime seeking a closer walk with the Lord through many trials and struggles against all-but-insurmountable obstacles. At last her faith was known around the world—a fact attested to by the hundreds of telegrams that poured in at the time of her death.

At the graveside services, it was my privilege to relate the account of what an inspiration Ethel Waters had been to me, particularly the last time I'd seen her. In 1974 I visited her in Los Angeles, while there for a Home Interiors' rally. At that time, Ethel was in low spirits, almost blinded by cataracts, living alone. I took her some nourishing food, but found her so weak that she could hardly hold a fork in her hand. I spent some time with her and assisted her with her meal, grateful for the privilege of having some time alone with someone I'd admired so much.

After dinner this dear Christian lady went and sat by a window overlooking the bright lights of the city. Soon she began to sing in a beautiful, high, sweet voice:

I'm going to LIVE the way HE wants me to live—
I'm going to GIVE until there's just no more to give,
I'm going to LOVE—LOVE 'til there's just no more love,
I could never, never outlove the LORD—

I COULD NEVER OUTLOVE THE LORD. Words by William J. and Gloria Gaither and Music by William J. Gaither. © Copyright 1972 by William J. Gaither. International copyright secured. All rights reserved. Used by permission.

It was the first time I'd ever heard Bill and Gloria Gaither's joyous song of commitment and my heart overflowed to hear it coming from the voice of such a valiant servant of God.

Ethel truly knew how to give of self, to share her talent and her faith. And God rewarded her with the ability to be a great witness for Him, to be instrumental in leading others to Christ. He blessed her with friends, fame, and vitality for many years, until at last He was ready to take her to her eternal home. Her story beautifully illustrates how God can turn even defeat into victory and blessings and joy for many, when it is committed to Him in faith.

God Himself is our Source. Anyone He chooses may be our supply. If the supply is shut off in one area, we must not panic or fear, but only remember to look to our Source. He who ". . . is able to do exceeding *abundantly* above all that we can ask or think, according to the power that worketh in us" (Ephesians 3:20 KJV, *italics mine*), is certainly able to find another avenue of supply for the blessings He wants to give His children. Our trust is in Him.

If we lean on Him completely and make a commitment to Him of all we are and all we possess, remembering that He has told us that the firstfruits belong to Him, we too will know the rewards that only He can give. In addition, we will know the joy of giving all the glory to Him!

The first step to this commitment is "realizing that God loves us and has a reason for our existence" as Nancy Thomas, senior manager, discovered. Share with Nancy her experience:

The wonder of God's plan for my life was to lose myself in something bigger than I was, so that I would have to turn to Him for guidance.

My job as a manager was His plan. When I began to really feel accepted by God's love, I realized that, even with His knowing all my sins and weaknesses, yet He still loved me in a very special way.

Mary Crowley's and Don Carter's faith in me, in their example to trust in the Lord, always leads me back to Proverbs for guidance in helping others.

As His child, we should remember:

God is your Father—Call home!

"My training manual is God's Word," so says Donna Mauricio, a branch manager in the Washington, D.C., area—a wife, mother, and successful career woman. Here is her testimony to the effectiveness of God's training manual:

Being part of the Home Interiors family for the past ten years is one of my greatest joys! I don't just have a job–I have a whole new way of life. Because of Mary Crowley's living Christian example, I, too, have come to know our Lord and have continued to grow personally and spiritually under her leadership. Where else can you go to work and study the Bible!

How glorious it is to know that my training manual is God's Word! That does give me a deep sense of security.

Why have I been so blessed? So that I can be a blessing to others. I know that Mary has spent much time, effort, and money helping me to grow and I, in turn, feel the responsibility to do no less for as many others as I can reach–and, hopefully, they too will reach others–and they others–and they still others–and as you can see, God's love can be spread so beautifully and reach so many because of one woman's effort.

I am grateful she cared . . . .

Grand Canyon College, Phoenix, Arizona. Mary C receiving Honorary Doctor's Degree, November 1977. *Below:* Managers, Janece Long, Marrilee Baker, Erlma Nelson, Darlene Wells, Jan Pinnow. Bob Kornegay Photography.

Mary C and managers. Bob Kornegay Photography. *Right:* Queen Elaine Jean and husband Paul. Bob Kornegay Photography.

Group picture. *Seated:* Barbara Hammond, Nancy Good, Nita Barker, Pearl Burns, Beverly Channell with Mary C. *Standing behind:* Shirley Buckalew, Dixie Haworth. Bob Kornegay Photography. *Below:* Luz Reynante and family (husband Rick), Queen of Queens 1976, National Queen 1975. Betty Byrum and husband Harold, 1977 seminar National Queen of Displayers 1976. Bob Kornegay Photography.

Dr. W. A. Criswell, Billy and Ruth Graham, Mrs. W. A. Criswell and Mary C. Bob Kornegay Photography. *Below:* In the plane for Montreat, N.C., March 1977. Mary and her winners in her private jet.

HOME INTERIORS

Mary C and her managers at 1977 seminar. Bob Kornegay Photography. *Right:* Tom Landry, Billy Graham, Mary C, Don Carter and Aunt Ruth Clark, Mary's auntie who is 83 years young. Bob Kornegay Photography.

Roger Staubach, Randy Hughes, Bob Breunig signing cowboy hats at Don Carter's ranch party. Bob Kornegay Photography. *Right:* Bob Hope giving Mary C a big hug for "Oscar" at Twentieth Anniversary celebration. Bob Kornegay Photography.

Mary C and dog Samantha at home. Bob Kornegay Photography. *Below:* Mary C autographing THINK MINK at seminar. Bob Kornegay Photography.

Mary Crowley at The First
Baptist Church, Dallas. Dr.
W. A. Criswell leads
applause. Bob Kornegay
Photography. *Right:* Mary
Crowley receiving award at
the Horatio Alger Award
Banquet, Waldorf-Astoria
Hotel, New York, May 1978.
Shown here with Dr. Nor-
man Vincent Peale.

Home Interiors managers and friends at Horatio Alger Award Banquet. *Right:* Mary C pictured here with the coveted Horatio Alger Award.

16

The Miracles in My Life

Trust in your money and down you go! Trust in God and flourish as a tree!

Proverbs 11:28

No one knows the truth of this verse in Proverbs more than one who has found himself in need of something no amount of money can buy. How true it is that the most precious things in life cannot be bought with silver or gold! And yet we so often take for granted the miracles of life and love and health and safety, not really appreciating them at all—until they are in jeopardy.

How can I ever forget the night of December 28, 1977? Still basking in the afterglow of the Christmas holiday, I waited at home to hear that my children, Don and Linda, and their children, Joey, Ronnie, and Christi, had returned home safely from a skiing trip to Montana.

Don had called earlier in the day to say that they were taking off in their plane from Pueblo, Colorado, and expected to reach Dallas at about 6 P.M. Although Don is an excellent pilot, I was still concerned about the weather, which was rainy, with intermittent fog, and definitely not good flying weather. Don had assured me that it was supposed to get better, but it did not clear, and by late afternoon the clouds just seemed to lower to the ground. Knowing that an instrument landing would be necessary, I was filled with apprehension. And so it was with a feeling of real relief that I answered the phone, when it rang at six-thirty, and blurted with a sigh, "Don! You're home!"

But it wasn't Don. Rather, it was his assistant, Don Breedlove, and he got right to the point. "Well, yes—they're in. But they landed off the runway. Joey and Christi are unhurt, but Linda is a little shook up. Don and Ronnie are scratched up some. They've been taken to Medical City Hospital emergency.''

Although his remarks turned out to be quite an understatement, his calm voice was encouraging. I drove serenely to the hospital, while thanking the Lord for His protective shield around my family. I felt very much relieved.

Only when I reached the emergency rooms did I begin to realize that the situation was far more serious than I'd realized. Linda was lying in one room, shaking with shock, her eye getting blacker by the minute. In another room lay Ronnie, a slash across the top of his head. Behind firmly closed doors in a third room, doctors worked over Don.

After what seemed an eternity, the neurologist came in and spoke to me. ''Mr. Carter's condition is critical,'' he said bluntly. ''We may have to do brain surgery. If that is the case, I want you to understand that there is some risk of infection. Unfortunately, antibiotics do not have an effect on this type of infection.''

All the strength drained out of me as the doctor spoke. A cry of protest welled up inside me but never reached my lips. I could only remember that it was merely a few hours since I'd talked to Don by phone, and he'd been fine then. Then my world had been safe and secure and far beyond the pale of disaster. Now, only a few hours later, the grim reality of tragedy hovered over me like a black cloud, abruptly and irrevocably obliterating the lingering joy of the holiday season. Summoning all my determination, I mentally cancelled out the negative words of the doctor and quietly placed my son in the loving hands of our Heavenly Father.

Later Don's family doctor arrived and told me that while Don's condition was critical, it was not necessarily fatal. Don was to be taken to surgery where the compound fracture of his ankle and his foot would be cleaned and set. His jaws and his teeth would be wired together temporarily, and a tracheotomy would be performed so that he would not choke on the blood from his facial injuries.

I asked the doctor if I might see Don briefly before he went to the operating room. At first he seemed reluctant, until I assured him that I would not upset my son by becoming emotional in his presence. When I entered the room where Don lay so broken and bloody, our dear Heavenly Father wrapped His strong arms around us both. I took Don's hand and felt his fingers clasp mine weakly. He managed to hang on to consciousness with grim determination, as he tried to talk to me. Motioning him to silence, I prayed with him and felt the calm assurance of God's love and power immediately strengthening and sustaining us both.

What a miracle prayer is! God is so great, so mighty! Never should we be afraid to ask Him for a miracle! Again and again in His Word He tells us to call upon Him and He promises to answer. He promises never to leave us or forsake us; that He is with us always; that He hears our faintest cry; that He is touched with the feelings of our infirmities; that our names are written on the palms of His hands. We are told to cast all our cares upon Him. His Word says that it is not possible for us to drift beyond His love and care. How comforting is His Word!

By the next day I learned that people all over the world were praying for Don and his family. From Johnny Cash's home in Jamaica, Billy and Ruth Graham called to assure me of their prayers. Paul Jay, a dear supplier friend, called from Italy. I heard from Dolph Sebell in Syracuse, New York, and Floyd and Millie Lyons got in touch by short wave from Peru. My beloved pastor, Dr. Criswell, and our minister of music, Gary Moore, came and stayed as did many others from our church. Prayer groups from the church and from Home Interiors' households all over the nation held special prayer vigils for Don around the clock, as the miracle of love and prayer continued to sustain us.

The loving support of those who care in time of need is a miracle indeed. Through them we feel God's compassionate touch in time of sorrow. What a great blessing to have the kind of friends who can be counted on to bear us up on wings of love and prayer in time of trouble—who can serve as channels for God's love and mercy.

But people, no matter how great their desire, are limited. They cannot always be there. Sometimes, even when they are present, they are helpless and frustrated at their inability to do more. We all have our human limitations.

I am so thankful that there is One who is not limited in any sense. He is the all-powerful Help of the helpless, the Fount of every blessing, the Source of all love and consolation. He is the Lord and Giver of life, the Son of Righteousness with healing in His wings. He heals the brokenhearted, binds up the afflicted, and sets at liberty those who are bruised. He is the Refuge of the weary, and He neither slumbers nor sleeps. His name is Jesus, and He is from everlasting to everlasting!

At last Don's status was changed from critical to serious. Miraculously, the brain surgery was not necessary. Linda and Ronnie healed gradually, as God performed His miracle of restoration in each one. By the time of the Twentieth Anniversary celebration in April, Don was able to walk with a cane. To the cheers of more than eleven thousand, he was able to stand before a microphone and laugh and make jokes. Surely there has been no greater miracle in my life than this one which made our Twentieth Anniversary celebration a double portion of blessing!

We can all expect to experience suffering in this life, and no amount of money can save us from it. Many of us are led to the Lord through suffering to begin with. Suffering need not be a waste, for if we trust in God, He is able to turn sorrow around and to bring blessings out of it. From our sorrow can spring a deeper relationship with Him—one in which we will experience His love and mercy in a deeper dimension than would have been possible otherwise.

There have been other equally real but less dramatic miracles in my life. Every miracle is born in the heart of God. So I call the first miracle the *Miracle of Birth*. That Mary Crowley should be born in Missouri, USA, on April 1, 1915, is a miracle. I could have been born in Russia or India, Peru, or some part of deepest Africa. Through God's miracle, I was born in America, where I would have an opportunity to become. I would have an opportunity to be free—an opportunity to use the free-enterprise system. And I was born to believing parents. Yes, my mother died when I was a year and a half old, but I was fortunate to be taken by my grandparents for the first five years of my life. These godly, stable, hard-working people gave me the rich inheritance of faith in God, as I daily witnessed their faith in action. I remember seeing my grandfather, as he came in after hail had ruined some crops, and he was singing "Have Thine Own Way, Lord"—not that the Lord sent the hail but that God would take that situation and make it work in our lives for good.

The second miracle is the *Love of God* that I learned as a child. During the time I lived with my father and stepmother—a family that I did not know—for six and a half years, the only friend that I had was Jesus. Many times I cried and I would talk to Him. He was my teacher. Those were tough times, but through it all He loved me. To me it's still a miracle that He loves me. It is the *greatest* miracle.

Then the *Miracle of Open Doors*. This came about as I had the responsibility of rearing two children and I came to Dallas, Texas. It is a miracle that God chose Dallas for me—because Dallas is a free-enterprise city. If you can cut it, you can do something great. There are not any cliques, prejudices. I was fortunate to have come to Dallas.

I made my way to First Baptist Church. That, too, was a miracle—

that there were people who loved and shared and took the time to care.

In the providence of time, when I was building a company for someone else, I suffered a great disappointment. God miraculously opened up all the doors for a new beginning and saved me from the deadly crippling diseases: self-pity and resentment. He gave me courage and determination to start all over again. The result was that I went into business for myself, and Home Interiors and Gifts came into being. One by one, I went to suppliers in the marketplace. They said, "Mary, I will do whatever I can. You have a good reputation." Repetition builds reputation. When God opens doors, you get up and go through them.

Out of this new beginning came the *Miracle of Sharing*. Don, my son and partner, was a shareholder from our beginning in our garage, and Ruthie was a Displayer, who later moved to the East and opened it up to Home Interiors. At the end of our first year in business, the company showed a little profit—but not much. I had never been president of a company before, but I had seen other people get bonuses at Christmastime. I had always felt that if I ever had a business, my employees should receive bonuses. I decided that we would pay a bonus. And since we were a corporation, and since we made a profit, we were going to pay dividends to our stockholders.

Our accountant announced that we could not do that. I said, "Why not? I am the president." It was explained to me that if we paid dividends, we would not have any reserve. "Reserve?" I replied. "It all depends on what you call reserve. You call it money. We call it people." So we paid the dividends. We are the only company I ever heard of that paid a cash dividend following the first year of operation. We didn't have any cash left but we had *reserves*.

Even then, we somehow knew the miracle of sharing, even though we did not have an understanding of God's arithmetic.

And I still don't. I never could understand how Jesus could feed the multitudes with a little boy's lunch. All I know is that it was just enough for one little boy—until it was given to Jesus. Then, after He blessed it, it was enough to feed the thousands who had come to hear Him.

All of us who work for Home Interiors are very ordinary people, but God has touched us and enabled us to feed the multitudes who work with us in this company. I do not understand just how, but I am grateful that He has.

I am grateful. I thank God for the miracles in my life, the ones in the past and the others still to come. Work is a blessing and wealth is a blessing, but the Book of Proverbs has something to say about real wealth.

> The Lord's blessing is our greatest wealth. All our work adds nothing to it!
>
> Proverbs 10:22

It's as true today as it was in the days of King Solomon. I am grateful that I have never been so hampered by education that I do not know how to believe God's Word and use it as a Source of wisdom. I am thankful that I can say that my God is a God of miracles. He is a God who can make life more joyous in the family, the home, and the world—on the job and in all life's other relationships!

17

Prayer Fountains

Reverence for the Lord is a fountain of life; its waters keep a man from death.

Proverbs 14:27

One of the greatest joys of my career has been due to the close relationships I have formed with others who work for Home Interiors. Many of us are more than just co-workers. Lots of us are prayer partners.

Sometimes I do not see my vice-president and friend, Barbara Hammond, for a week at a time. And I do not see my good friend Pearl Burns, who lives many miles away. Others, too, do not frequently cross my path. Yet I know that I can call them at any hour of the day or night, and we can immediately become one in the Spirit. When we need help or want to share a joy or a sorrow—or even a problem—we don't have to go back and review the whole story, because we already know each other at a deeper level than most business people ever do. We are always praying for one another.

Such human relationships are especially precious and rewarding, but even more wonderful is my relationship with my Lord. I can call Him collect any time, anywhere. My real Boss is never out and His line is never busy. He is never tied up and unavailable. I think God's switchboard must look much like the charts used by computer programmers that Dave used to bring home from his office. The grid of lines, representing the pathways by which messages are transmitted, looks like a maze of tangled thread in an untidy sewing basket. The lines in God's switchboard must number in the billions; yet every single line gets through to Him!

But we can put things on our lines that keep our messages from being transmitted to God. Ice can break lines. Perhaps we have let our lines freeze because we haven't had any warm communication with Him for a long time. Possibly there are innocent-looking little birds sitting on our lines and causing interference. Self-pity, resentment, unforgiveness, bitterness, doubt—these all garble our messages. Fear is another nonconductor that keeps God's love from getting through to us.

How do we rid ourselves of the obstacles that hinder God's messages? We pray about them often, asking God to help us. We try to change our attitudes and our behavior, one little area at a time. As we do this, we thank Him for helping us. Sometimes we can even thank Him in advance for what He is going to do. "I know You are going to do something great today," we may pray. God likes to hear that. He has told us so. We must expect great things to happen in our lives.

> Reverence for the Lord is a fountain of life; its waters keep a man from death.
>
>   Proverbs 14:27

If we have reverence for the Lord, and if we value our relationship with Him, then we will spend a special time each day with Him in prayer. As we yield ourselves daily to Him in this way, seeking His face and bringing our praise, thanksgiving, and petitions, He will, in turn, shower us with blessings.

Someone once asked me, "Don't you think you might be bothering God with all the requests you make to Him for the things that aren't really so important? After all, He has more to think about than all the little details of *your* life."

It was my privilege to explain to this person that God delights in hearing from us and that we cannot bother Him too much. Because He is a loving Father, it gives Him great joy when His children come away from other interests for a special time alone with Him. In His Word He encourages us to ask, to seek, to knock. He promises that He will always answer us.

In prayer, our relationship with our Heavenly Father is forged as in no other way. Jesus was always in contact with His Father. The Scriptures admonish us to pray without ceasing. This means that we are always to be in an attitude of prayer, so that the lines of communication with God are constantly open. Those who are obedient will find God speaking to them at the most unexpected times and places and in the most unusual ways. Yet His voice is always recognizable to those who are diligent in prayer. Our understanding of self, our victory over self, and our ministry to others can never be any greater than our prayer life.

> In everything you do, put God first, and he will direct you and crown your efforts with success.
>
> Proverbs 3:6

Every one of us who has come to the Lord has undoubtedly prayed something like this: "Lord, I want You to take control of my life. I want You to be my Savior. I accept the gift of salvation and I thank You, Lord. *Amen.*" (If you have never yet prayed to God in this way and you would like to begin a new life of joy and victory, you may want to stop reading and do so right now.)

When we ask God to come into our lives and rule our hearts, we receive the gift of salvation. We are *saved,* but we must grow in grace. Such growth is a continuous process which progresses throughout our entire lives. Every day we must start over again, working on this process minute by minute, hour by hour. Although we are saved, we still are in the flesh, and we will have constant struggles with our sin nature as long as we live.

> There are two natures in my breast;
> One is foul, one is blest.
> One I love, one I hate,
> The one I feed will dominate.

This little poem explains very well the necessity of feeding on the Word of God. We must nurture the divine nature in ourselves and develop it. The obstacles to spiritual growth are many, and only daily prayer can overcome them.

I have so loved the four-point prayer exercise Barbara Hammond's pastor recommended that I want to share it. It isn't easy to follow. The pastor himself admitted that it was difficult for him to do the four things that he was recommending. For those who do them faithfully every day, however, the rewards are many.

1. *Spend the first two minutes after you wake up every morning in gratitude to God.* (If you don't do it the very first thing, you probably won't have the uninterrupted time later.) Be grateful until you fairly

glow. Gratitude is the heart's memory. No one can be grateful and unhappy at the same time.

How can you be grateful when things are not going well? Well, you might say, "Lord, I thank You that I woke up this morning." Or you might say, "Thank You that I can get up. Thank You that I have meaningful work to do, and that I have health, a good mind, eyes with which to see."

2. *Make your mealtime grace special rather than just ordinary and routine.* At one meal have each member of the family say at least one thing for which he or she is thankful; or, in the morning, each member might ask for help for one particular need that day. Don't ever let a mealtime blessing become a meaningless ritual.

3. *Replace frustration and anger with prayer.* These emotions are the hardest to overcome, because they involve our relationships to others. When you feel yourself becoming frustrated, start praying instead of reacting. You can pray mentally in the presence of others. If nothing else, you can say, "Lord, help me to keep my mouth shut, and my ears and heart open."

Keep prayed up. Pray each other up, even those who are frustrating you. Pray for your entire list of people and for their needs each day. God is interested in every detail of our life and theirs, so praying is the most important thing you can do.

An old man and his grandson were once hiking in a field, when the farmer's bull started barreling down on them. Both began to run. Suddenly the boy shouted, "Grandfather, don't you think we ought to stop and pray?"

"Not now," the grandfather shouted back. "I keep prayed up for times like this!"

Keep prayed up for the really difficult times that are sure to come, because they come to us all.

When you pray for others, you will see them changing right before your eyes. They will not know why their attitudes are changing, but they will, nevertheless. God will knock at the doors of their hearts in answer to your prayer. There are so many people all around us with deep hurts. The only way we can help many of them is to turn them over to God and let Him care for them. When we open our minds and hearts to God, He will give us wisdom to know the things to do that will help.

4. *Review the day with God at bedtime.* Find a private place to do this. Sometimes the bathroom is the only place you can go to shut out the rest of the family. For at least ten minutes, talk to God openly and freely about the happenings of the day. Confess your failures. Thank Him for the ways in which He helped you to succeed. Ask for His help for tomorrow. If you review your day with God, you can then close out the matter and not carry the failures of one day over into the next. You can leave your mistakes with Him and rest while He works on all the problems you've brought to Him. You can entrust to Him your own trials and those of your loved ones, knowing that He can and will do something about them while you rest.

God has ways that are beyond our understanding, and He knows the end from the beginning. He is able to take the most disastrous of circumstances and turn them around for His glory and for our good. He can truly make something beautiful, something good, out of the brokenness of our lives, when we yield to Him in faith. Often He must allow us to be broken before He can remold us in His image. It is not ours to question why; He is the Potter and we are only the clay. It is enough to know that the Potter is able to form a vessel to His liking out of this unwieldly lump of human clay—one that will then reflect the glory of the treasure within, as we are daily filled with Him.

I am reminded of my precious friend, Kim Wickes, who was blinded at the age of three by a bomb in Korea. Kim could have become bitter and thus been handicapped throughout her life. Instead, she had hope. Kim was brought to America and was adopted by a wonderful American family. She learned to live by the promise in Isaiah: "And He shall make darkness light" (*see* Isaiah 42:16). When Kim grew up she wanted to develop her musical talent. Through the help of Cliff Barrows and Billy Graham, she was able to receive musical training here in America and later obtained a scholarship to study voice in Vienna. This beautiful young woman traveled alone to a foreign country and, despite her blindness, studied and lived there, taking complete care of herself. I first met her in Lausanne, Switzerland, where she sang for the Congress on Evangelism in 1974. Later she came back to America and we became friends.

Kim sang before the Home Interiors' Twentieth Anniversary celebration and I could not help but marvel at the way in which God had brought victory out of tragedy for her. Her beautiful face was radiant with the joy of serving the Lord. As her rich voice filled the auditorium, she was indeed a living testimony to the power of God to overcome human imperfection.

In time of sorrow we are often too numb or too weak to have faith. Some days we may be just too tired to make the effort. How wonderful to know that our faith does not depend on us, but on the One who gives it. Its effectiveness is not in how much we can work up, but rather in the reliability of the Person in whom we put our faith. Faith misplaced, no matter how strong, is wasted. Look at the people who zealously put their faith in Hitler and in his master race and the hope of world conquest. Their faith was strong, but it was misplaced. In the end, they were left without hope. Faith in God is never misplaced, never wasted. He is able to turn even our fears into faith, when we give them to Him. Elton Trueblood said, "Faith is fear that has said its prayers."

What security there is in knowing that our faith does not depend on us but that it is a gift from God. In times of weakness we do not need to feel condemned because we don't have enough faith; we merely take our weakness to the Lord. That alone is an act of faith, and He will honor our obedience by renewing and increasing in us daily this precious gift.

Prayer is a mighty weapon, and an abiding faith is the result of diligent prayer. Jesus prayed often, and He taught His disciples to pray. The Scriptures tell us that much is accomplished by fervent prayer. We must learn to think of prayer not as a last resort—as many do—but as a *first* resource. Instead of spinning our wheels and wearing ourselves out with worry and anxiety, we need to learn to rest in the Lord and pray in faith, believing. God doesn't always do things our way, but it is because He knows our real needs better than we do. If He does not give us what we ask for, He will always give us something that is far better for us.

When we do not know how to pray, when we cannot find the words, we have the assurance that the Holy Spirit helps us to form acceptable prayers to the Father. Prayer is not always words. A beloved hymn of the church tells us that prayer is sometimes merely a heavy sigh, a falling tear, a look toward heaven. Often it is utter silence, in which the desire of the heart is communicated without speech. Sometimes it is merely the knowledge that God readies our hearts more than He listens to our words. He hears. He understands. He answers.

> Oh, Thou by whom we come to God,
> The Life, the Truth, the Way,

The path of prayer Thyself hast trod.
Lord, teach us how to pray!

May I share with you one of my very favorite poems—it speaks to my heart:

Dear Child,
God does not say to you today, "Be strong"—
He knows your strength is spent—
He knows how long the road has been—
How weary you've become, for
He who walked this earth alone—
Each boggy lowland and each rugged hill, understands—
And so He simply says, "Be still,
Be still and know that I am God."
The hour is late and you must rest awhile—
Let life's reservoirs fill up, as slow rain
    fills an empty upturned cup.
Hold up your cup, dear Child, for God to fill.
He only asks that you be still.

AUTHOR UNKNOWN

18

God's Liberation for Women

*It is possible to give away and become richer! It is also possible
to hold on too tightly and lose everything. Yes, the liberal man
shall be rich. By watering others, he waters himself.*

Proverbs 11:24, 25

One of the most exciting experiences of my life was in receiving the
Doctor of Laws degree from Grand Canyon College in Phoenix in
November 1976. This event came about as the result of my having
spoken to an organization of college presidents on the subject of
motivating people to support Christian education. It was a very special
honor—and a most unexpected one—for one who'd never had the
opportunity to complete her higher education. In addition, it was a
fresh reminder that God gives grace to the humble!

As I sat waiting to receive this honor, I could not help but reflect on
the fact that women today are being urged to become aggressive and
assertive, hard and domineering, masculine and cold—just so that they
can win more honors and compete with men in the marketplace.

How sad! And how ridiculous! God never intended woman to be
equal to man, and the only way that she can do so is to lower herself.
Even then it is physically impossible for woman to be man's equal,
because there are just too many differences between men and women.
Quite a few of us are still praising God for the difference!

What can we women do while the talk shows blare away at us, and
the magazine articles exhort us repeatedly to come out of ourselves and
become assertive and demanding? We can go back to God's Word, to
the Book of Proverbs.

Trust in the Lord with all thine heart, and lean not unto thine own understanding.

Proverbs 3:5 KJV

If we really know God and trust Him, we will lean on His understanding and not that of some twentieth-century self-appointed expert, usually female, who didn't have sense enough to know when she was well off to begin with. If our focus is on reverence for God, rather than on hostility toward men, we will have a true understanding of His purpose for us. As we see ourselves made in His image, we will also see that He has endowed us with certain attributes and characteristics which enable us to fulfill His design for our lives. We will then know that we cannot act effectively apart from His plan for our lives, and that to attempt to do so would be unnatural and damaging.

Our Heavenly Father has endowed us women with certain special qualities that men do not possess in the same degree. Men are logical and women are intuitive. Men have physical strength, but women have endurance. Men are usually deliberate and businesslike, while women are inclined to be tender and compassionate. Men build things that will function and women create things of beauty. Both are necessary and good, and both complement each other because they were meant to do so as part of the divine plan.

It is neither wise nor safe to thwart God's divine plan, either for individuals or for nations. When women persist in demanding their rights, they may very well get what they demand. Yet God intended for woman to have so much more than mere rights. In demanding and attaining her rights, she loses something far more precious. She steps out of the realm of the special and into the category of the ordinary.

Is it possible, many will ask, for a woman to excel as a woman and not worry about rights? A good answer to that question can be found in the statement which one of our Home Interiors' managers, Beverly Channell, made concerning her career in our Twentieth Anniversary book. As an area manager, Beverly is among the top six executives in our company and a leader of thousands of other women in the business. Beverly wrote:

The most important decision we have to make in life is not what we want to be, but what kind of life we want to live. I could never have imagined the abundance of living that lay in store for me, once that decision was made. I feel that it is more than mere coincidence that I was led to inquire into home decorating. I firmly believe that God has a plan for each of us, and that He is just waiting for us to commit our ways unto Him.

To watch the fulfilled potential of the many lives which have been a part of the unfolding drama of the building of our company is the greatest reward of all. To see so many trusting in God's plan, believing in people, and sharing the methods of helping people help themselves just makes me want to pray for a greater capacity to contain the joy of it all!

Therein lies the real reason for our labor—not just to earn money, although God does want to reward us financially—but as a way of life, a way of serving others as Jesus served us—a way of enriching the lives of others by our endeavors, as He has blessed and enriched us. When we put our energies into loving others and bringing greater fulfillment to their lives, instead of worrying about our own rights, we are truly liberated. We then become free to enjoy our labors and to enjoy the fruits thereof. Instead of souring the family with our ambitions, we rather enrich it. We are able to grow without growing away from those we love.

Twenty-six-year-old Nanci Hammond, daughter of our vice-president, wrote a letter for our Twentieth Anniversary in which she thanked us for all that her mother's career had meant to her. She shared with us that her mother had very wisely permitted her to be a part of the business, had allowed her to help unpack orders, and had encouraged her to meet the guests. While growing up, Nanci had attended the Home Interiors' seminars and had heard one speaker after another give God the glory for her own success.

"These are just a few of the many things that stand out in my mind," Nanci wrote. "But there is something much greater. It's what Home Interiors has done for my mom. Watching my mom grow has been the best part. To see her develop into the super lady that she is has been a great encouragement to me in my own career. She is a dynamic businesswoman and a good friend. But best of all, she's my mom."

These wonderful accomplishments didn't just happen. Barbara Hammond and Beverly Channell, like many other successful yet feminine and charming ladies, have learned the value of setting goals and changing their attitudes a bit at a time. They know that the love of God impels us to strive for higher goals in every area of our lives. They have learned that the surest way to find ourselves is to lose ourselves in something greater.

In May 1978, I was blessed to receive the Horatio Alger Award, an honor presented each year by Dr. Norman Vincent Peale to a group of Americans who are selected because of their purposeful hard work and their faith in the American system of free enterprise. A prerequisite is that these people must share their good fortune in such a way that jobs, health, and a higher standard of living are brought to others. The lives of the awardees must be an example of how our country affords real opportunity for success.

It was a real honor for me. At the reception before the awards, I met many former winners such as Lowell Thomas, Mrs. Helen Boehm of the Boehm porcelains, and others. Afterward, we fourteen in the Class of '78 went into the banquet hall to receive our trophies and each of us was given a lovely bust of Horatio Alger. It was an especially happy occasion for me, because in the audience were 110 of my Home Interiors' family, as well as my daughter, Ruth, and her family. After being introduced by Dr. Peale I had the opportunity to share some of my own thoughts about success.

"I think that one person with a belief is equal to a force of ninety-nine with only an interest," I said. "And I have a belief. I believe in the Creator who made me in His image. Because of that fact, I am somebody. Consequently, I am able to look at everybody else as somebody, too.

"I believe in hard work and in incentive. I think work is valuable to the person who does it, as well as to the people for whom it is done.

"I believe in women. I think women are pretty special. And I believe in America and in the free-enterprise system. I believe in the opportunities here in our country. And I know that when we dedicate ourselves to a purpose that will enrich the lives of others, and then work toward the fulfillment of that purpose, the rewards will come."

Many people do not realize that God wants to reward us. They talk about luck, pretending that if it were not for coincidence, they, too, would be successful. They make excuses for their failure. Others, however, are able to see the relationship between cause and effect and know that God does indeed reward our efforts, when they are dedicated to Him.

I like what jockey Willie Shoemaker said at the banquet: "The more dedication I work with, and the harder I work, the more luck I have." And it was Thomas Edison who said that success is 10 percent inspiration and 90 percent perspiration! Emerson said it in a different way: ''If you love and serve enough, you cannot possibly escape the remuneration.''

And I agree!

I am happy to say that I am a liberated woman. I have been liberated from want and failure by God Himself, and I am free indeed! He wants to do the same for every other woman. He wants to give each of us an abundance of peace and joy and a sense of worth and pride in accomplishment. And He can—if we will only learn to lean on Him and put Him first in everything that we do.

By His grace and with His help we can be Women Who Win!

This book has been written about ''women who win''—women who have done it through the teaching of Proverbs and the control of Jesus Christ. Yet the principles are applicable to men as well, and it is my hope that men who want to be leaders and who want to be winners will read this book too—and that all readers will be drawn more dearly to the loving Saviour and will develop a thirst for study of the Holy Word.

19

Power From Proverbs

Every young man who listens to me and obeys my instructions will be given wisdom and good sense. Yes, if you want better insight and discernment, and are searching for them as you would for lost money or hidden treasure, then wisdom will be given you, and knowledge of God himself; you will soon learn the importance of reverence for the Lord and of trusting him.

Proverbs 2:1–5

Intelligence can produce knowledge, but only God can grant wisdom which is the ability and skill to serve Him in daily living. God's Word is:

> the traveler's map
> the pilot's compass
> the pilgrim's staff
> the soldier's sword
> the believer's "log book."

The Bible contains:

> Light to direct you
> Comfort to console you
> Food to sustain you
> Wisdom to teach you
> Fire to warm you.

This Book reveals the love of God.
This Book reveals the mind of God.

This Book reveals the state of man, the way of salvation, the doom of
the unrepentant. Its Author is God; its writers were men; its infalli-
bility inspired by God's Spirit.

> Read the Bible thoughtfully, prayerfully, daily.
> Read it to be wise.
> Believe it to be safe.
> Proclaim it to be holy.

Much of Proverbs is devoted to imparting the keys to being wise.
Each time I read in Proverbs, I am brought to a conscious realization
that the answers to specific problems are written—inspired by the wisdom of our Father—transmitted in phrases that amount to common
sense for the Christian. Proverbs constantly point out that it takes
instruction, discipline, and work to give us the skills to live our lives
beautifully and pleasing to God.

Often we feel that if we just had easy reference to these powerful
phrases, we could keep our problems and pressures in God's perspective. Proverbs are not promises however; rather they are examples and
admonitions. They do not propose to change the world, but rather
teach us how to have the skill to live in it.

Many years ago I discovered that the principles and precepts developed in the Book of Proverbs were really the foundation for the
wisdom of life, of business, of home—and more specifically *of becoming leaders.* So we started using the Book of Proverbs as our basic
training manual in our Mountain Retreat in Buena Vista, Colorado.
Each new manager was given a Living Bible, leather-bound with her
name on it, and each morning we would take a portion of Proverbs.
Each member of our learning school was to find examples in our desig-
nated chapter which spoke to her need for learning, and we would
study together. Through these many years, my own personal Living
Bible is a treasure house of pink underlined precepts, special bits of
wisdom within the margin that I have learned from my dear pastor and
other leaders; special dates that have been a time of blessing and reassurance in my own life and work. So as a summary of this book, I
would like to leave you with a quick, handy reference to the gems of
wisdom to be learned from the Book of Proverbs.

For your easy reference, the Book of Proverbs has been summarized
by category, listed alphabetically, and not in any range of importance.
(I've included some of the notes from my own Bible.)

Book of Proverbs (by Category)

ADVERSITY

You are a poor specimen if you can't stand the pressure of adversity.

Proverbs 24:10

AFFLICTION

Silver and gold are purified by fire, but God purifies hearts.

Proverbs 17:3

AMBITION

A man who loves pleasure becomes poor; wine and luxury are not the way to riches!

Proverbs 21:17

ARROGANCE

If anyone respects and fears God, he will hate evil. For wisdom hates pride, arrogance, corruption and deceit of every kind.

Proverbs 8:13

ATTITUDE

To learn, you must want to be taught. To refuse reproof is stupid.

Proverbs 12:1

When you work for God, the pay is good and the retirement is . . . "out of this world."

MCC

BEAUTY

A beautiful woman lacking discretion and modesty is like a fine gold ring in a pig's snout.

Proverbs 11:22

CHEATING

Ill-gotten gain brings no lasting happiness; right living does.

Proverbs 10:2

CHEERFULNESS
When a man is gloomy, everything seems to go wrong; when he is cheerful, everything seems right!

Proverbs 15:15

God blesses those who obey him; happy the man who puts his trust in the Lord.

Proverbs 16:20

A cheerful heart does good like medicine, but a broken spirit makes one sick.

Proverbs 17:22

CITIZENSHIP
The good influence of godly citizens causes a city to prosper, but the moral decay of the wicked drives it downhill.

Proverbs 11:11

COMMON SENSE
Have two goals: wisdom—that is, knowing and doing right—and common sense. Don't let them slip away.

Proverbs 3:21

COMMUNICATION
An unreliable messenger can cause a lot of trouble. Reliable communication permits progress.

Proverbs 13:17

COMPLAINING
A constant dripping on a rainy day and a cranky woman are much alike! You can no more stop her complaints than you can stop the wind or hold onto anything with oil-slick hands.

Proverbs 27:15, 16

CORRUPTION
If anyone respects and fears God, he will hate evil. For wisdom hates pride, arrogance, corruption and deceit of every kind.

Proverbs 8:13

CRITICISM
If you refuse criticism you will end in poverty and disgrace; if you accept criticism you are on the road to fame.

Proverbs 13:18

DEBTS

It is poor judgment to countersign another's note, to become responsible for his debts.

Proverbs 17:18

DECISIONS

For the Lord grants wisdom! His every word is a treasure of knowledge and understanding. He grants good sense to the godly—his saints. He is their shield, protecting them and guarding their pathway. He shows how to distinguish right from wrong, how to find the right decision every time.

Proverbs 2:6–9

Don't ever be afraid of tomorrow—God is already there.

MCC

DRINK

Wine gives false courage; hard liquor leads to brawls; what fools men are to let it master them, making them reel drunkenly down the street!

Proverbs 20:1

ENCOURAGEMENT

Anxious hearts are very heavy but a word of encouragement does wonders!

Proverbs 12:25

FAIRNESS

The Lord demands fairness in every business deal. He established this principle.

Proverbs 16:11

FAMILY

The fool who provokes his family to anger and resentment will finally have nothing worthwhile left. He shall be the servant of a wiser man.

Proverbs 11:29

FLATTERY

For the lips of a prostitute are as sweet as honey, and smooth flattery is her stock in trade.

Proverbs 5:3

FRIENDS
Be with wise men and become wise. Be with evil men and become evil.
Proverbs 13:20

GENEROSITY
Work hard and become a leader; be lazy and never succeed. Anxious hearts are very heavy but a word of encouragement does wonders!
Proverbs 12:24, 25

True humility and respect for the Lord lead a man to riches, honor and long life.

Proverbs 22:4

GOSSIP
Fire goes out for lack of fuel, and tensions disappear when gossip stops.

Proverbs 26:20

Gossip is sharing negative information about a person or a situation with someone who is neither a part of the problem nor the solution.

MCC

GREED
Greed causes fighting; trusting God leads to prosperity.

Proverbs 28:25

GRIPING
It is better to live in a corner of an attic than in a beautiful home with a cranky, quarrelsome woman.

Proverbs 25:24

Gentle words cause life and health; griping brings discouragement.

Proverbs 15:4

HERITAGE
It is a wonderful heritage to have an honest father.

Proverbs 20:7

HONOR
To do right honors God; to sin is to despise him.

Proverbs 14:2

HUMILITY

Humility and reverence for the Lord will make you both wise and honored.

Proverbs 15:33

HUSBAND

A worthy wife is her husband's joy and crown; the other kind corrodes his strength and tears down everything he does.

Proverbs 12:4

INSIGHT

Yes, if you want better insight and discernment, and are searching for them as you would for lost money or hidden treasure, then wisdom will be given you, and knowledge of God himself; you will soon learn the importance of reverence for the Lord and of trusting him.

Proverbs 2:3–5

JEALOUSY

Crooks are jealous of each other's loot, while good men long to help each other.

Proverbs 12:12

Some people like to make cutting remarks, but the words of the wise soothe and heal.

Proverbs 12:18

JOY

God blesses those who obey him; happy the man who puts his trust in the Lord.

Proverbs 16:20

If we work for the things we believe in—
We are rich, though the way is rough.
Work only for money—
And never get quite enough.

MCC

JUSTICE

A good man loves justice, but it is a calamity to evil-doers.

Proverbs 21:15

KINDNESS
Kind words are like honey—enjoyable and healthful.

Proverbs 16:24

KNOWLEDGE
For the Lord grants wisdom! His every word is a treasure of knowledge and understanding.

Proverbs 2:6

LAZINESS
Take a lesson from the ants, you lazy fellow. Learn from their ways and be wise! For though they have no king to make them work, yet they labor hard all summer, gathering food for the winter.

Proverbs 6:6, 7

Lazy men are soon poor; hard workers get rich.

Proverbs 10:4

LEADERSHIP
Without wise leadership, a nation is in trouble; but with good counselors there is safety.

Proverbs 11:14

Work hard and become a leader; be lazy and never succeed.

Proverbs 12:24

If you profit from constructive criticism you will be elected to the wise men's hall of fame. But to reject criticism is to harm yourself and your own best interests.

Proverbs 15:31, 32

LENDING
When you help the poor you are lending to the Lord—and he pays wonderful interest on your loan!

Proverbs 19:17

Unless you have the extra cash on hand, don't countersign a note. Why risk everything you own? They'll even take your bed!

Proverbs 22:26, 27

LOVE
Love forgets mistakes; nagging about them parts the best of friends.

Proverbs 17:9

LYING

For there are six things the Lord hates—no, seven:
  Haughtiness
  Lying
  Murdering
  Plotting evil
  Eagerness to do wrong
  A false witness
  Sowing discord among brothers

Proverbs 6:16–19

MORALITY

The upright are directed by their honesty; the wicked shall fall beneath their load of sins.

Proverbs 11:5

Godliness exalts a nation, but sin is a reproach to any people.

Proverbs 14:34

OBEDIENCE

When a man is trying to please God, God makes even his worst enemies to be at peace with him.

Proverbs 16:7

PATIENCE

Be patient and you will finally win, for a soft tongue can break hard bones.

Proverbs 25:15

PERCEPTIVENESS

Teach a wise man, and he will be the wiser; teach a good man, and he will learn more.

Proverbs 9:9

I DIDN'T HAVE TIME TO PRAY
I got up early one morning
And rushed right into the day,
I had so much to accomplish
That I did not have time to pray.

Problems just tumbled about me
And heavier came each task,

"Why doesn't God help me?"
I wondered and He answered, "You didn't ask."

I tried to come into God's presence
I used all my keys at the lock,
And God gently and lovingly chided,
"Why, child, you didn't knock."

I wanted to see joy and beauty
But the day toiled on gray and bleak,
I wondered why God didn't show me,
And He said, "You didn't seek."

I woke up early this morning
And paused before entering the day,
I had so much to accomplish
That I had to take time to pray.

AUTHOR UNKNOWN   MCC

PLANNING
We should make plans—counting on God to direct us.

Proverbs 16:9

A sensible man watches for problems ahead and prepares to meet them. The simpleton never looks, and suffers the consequences.

Proverbs 27:12

POVERTY
Work brings profit; talk brings poverty!

Proverbs 14:23

PRAISE
Don't praise yourself; let others do it!

Proverbs 27:2

PRIDE
Pride leads to arguments; be humble, take advice and become wise.

Proverbs 13:10

Pride ends in destruction; humility ends in honor.

Proverbs 18:12

PROFIT

An empty stable stays clean—but there is no income from an empty stable.

Proverbs 14:4

Any enterprise is built by wise planning, becomes strong through common sense, and profits wonderfully by keeping abreast of the facts.

Proverbs 24:3, 4

PROMISES

God delights in those who keep their promises, and abhors those who don't.

Proverbs 12:22

QUARRELING

It is hard to stop a quarrel once it starts, so don't let it begin.

Proverbs 17:14

REARING CHILDREN

Teach a child to choose the right path, and when he is older he will remain upon it.

Proverbs 22:6

Don't fail to correct your children; discipline won't hurt them! They won't die if you use a stick on them! Punishment will keep them out of hell.

Proverbs 23:13, 14

RELATIONSHIPS

It is harder to win back the friendship of an offended brother than to capture a fortified city. His anger shuts you out like iron bars.

Proverbs 18:19

REVERENCE

Reverence for God adds hours to each day; so how can the wicked expect a long, good life?

Proverbs 10:27

Better a little with reverence for God, than great treasure and trouble with it.

Proverbs 15:16

RICHES

Your riches won't help you on Judgment Day; only righteousness counts then.

Proverbs 11:4

SELF-CONTROL
Self-control means controlling the tongue! A quick retort can ruin everything.

Proverbs 13:3

SKILL
Evil words destroy. Godly skill rebuilds.

Proverbs 11:9

SUCCESS
The whole city celebrates a good man's success—and also the godless man's death.

Proverbs 11:10

Commit your work to the Lord, then it will succeed.

Proverbs 16:3

TEMPER
A wise man restrains his anger and overlooks insults. This is to his credit.

Proverbs 19:11

Honor the Lord by giving him the first part of all your income, and he will fill your barns with wheat and barley and overflow your wine vats with the finest wines.

Proverbs 3:9, 10

TRUTH
Telling the truth gives a man great satisfaction, and hard work returns many blessings to him.

Proverbs 12:14

Some men die by shrapnel—
Some go down in flames,
But most men perish inch by inch,
Playing at little games.

MCC

UNDERSTANDING
For the reverence and fear of God are basic to all wisdom. Knowing God results in every other kind of understanding.

Proverbs 9:10

WIFE
A worthy wife is her husband's joy and crown; the other kind corrodes his strength and tears down everything he does.

Proverbs 12:4

WISDOM
Every young man who listens to me and obeys my instructions will be given wisdom and good sense. Yes, if you want better insight and discernment, and are searching for them as you would for lost money or hidden treasure, then wisdom will be given you, and knowledge of God himself; you will soon learn the importance of reverence for the Lord and of trusting him.

Proverbs 2:1–5

How does a man become wise? The first step is to trust and reverence the Lord!

Proverbs 1:7, 8

The Wisdom Literature more often speaks of scheming women than it does of lustful men.

MCC

WOMAN
A wise woman builds her house, while a foolish woman tears hers down by her own efforts.

Proverbs 14:1

While Proverbs is full of inspired writings which are powerful in their influence on our lives, they do not have the power to change lives, nor can the reading of them keep us constantly motivated to live victorious lives. Only Jesus Christ provides such power. The eloquent words of Dr. Shadrach Meshach Lockridge describe the Source of Power in our lives:

Men have tried to destroy Him . . .
But don't you know you can't destroy Him?

What would you use for Power?

All power belongs to Him!

If you try to destroy Him by rejecting or ignoring Him—

Before you know it—you will hear a still small voice saying:

> "Behold, I stand at the door and knock—if any man hear my voice and open the door, I will come in to him, and will sup with him—and he with me."

If you try to destroy Him by fire He will refuse to burn—

If you try to destroy Him by water, He will walk on the water.

If you try to destroy Him by a strong wind, the tempest will lick His hand and lay down at His feet.

If you try to destroy Him with the law—you will find no fault in Him.

If you try to destroy Him with the seal of an empire—He will break it!

If you try to destroy Him by putting Him in a grave—HE WILL ARISE!

At His birth, men came from the East. At His death, men came from the West and the East and West met in Him. HE IS LORD. HALLELUJAH—and the Lord Omnipotent Reigneth!

EPILOGUE

A really good woman is very difficult to find, for she is as rare as a precious stone, and far more valuable. Her husband is able to trust her completely in every way, so that he never has the need to demand or force her to do anything. He knows that everything she does will always be for his good. She is willing—even glad—to work creatively and industriously with her hands. She tries to think of ways to provide good, nutritious meals for her household and plans ahead in order to save money. She makes a wise investment of the money she has saved for the prosperity of her family. She is careful to get plenty of exercise and to guard her health. She knows the value of her goods and services and makes sure that they are quality. She plans from day to day, and nothing goes to waste while she sleeps. She is not afraid to devote herself to creativity and industry for the good of her family, and out of her abundance, she shares gladly with those less fortunate. Cold weather is no threat to her, for she has spent her time wisely in preparing for it, and all her family will be clothed warmly and attractively because of her intelligent planning and hard work. She, too, will be clad in attractive attire. Because of her own good reputation, her husband is well respected everywhere he goes. She devotes a portion of her time to challenges and interests which fulfill her and at the same time bring a profit. She can be counted on to be strong and honorable at all times, and she possesses a quiet, inner confidence, which gives her great joy and peace of mind in all circumstances. Her words are wise and prudent, and she never says anything unkind about anyone. She is always busy taking care of her home and family, and she will never be found wasting time. Her children think she is wonderful, and they tell her so. Her husband also loves and admires her and tells her that she is the best woman in the world. Even though she may not necessarily be the prettiest woman in town, she will have a special beauty because of her reverence for the Lord and joy in living. She will be loved because of it. She will reap exactly what she has sown—a rich harvest of love and mercy, security and praise.

Proverbs 31:10–30 (*paraphrased*)